A Link to the

Engaging Students in the Study of History

MICHAEL M. YELL
GEOFFREY SCHEURMAN
WITH KEITH REYNOLDS

NCSS
Bulletin 102

National Council for the Social Studies

8555 Sixteenth Street • Suite 500 • Silver Spring, Maryland 20910

www.**socialstudies**.org

Editorial staff on this publication: Steven S. Lapham, Drew Saunders, Michael Simpson
Art Director/Production: Gene Cowan

Library of Congress Control Number: 2004108088
ISBN: 0-87986-096-0

Printed in the United States of America

5 4 3 2 1

Contents

To Our Families

ANN, RYAN, ALYSSA, AND AARON YELL

MARCIA, JENNIFER, STEPHEN, AND KENYON SCHEURMAN

CHRISTOPHER REYNOLDS

Preface

MICHAEL M. YELL

This August, I will begin my twenty-ninth year as a social studies teacher. My experience has shown me the importance of having a solid repertoire of thoughtful and engaging instructional strategies that involve students in the subject matter of history. Strategies that get students discussing, thinking, writing and interacting with the content are invaluable for helping them learn and understand that content. Through such strategies, the teacher can create a classroom environment that is thoughtful, active, and conducive to learning.

The strategies outlined in this book have the purpose of not only engaging students in the study of history, but of helping them to explore and think about the content, the ideas, and the concepts that they encounter. The book is organized into six chapters outlining teaching strategies, one chapter with in-depth lesson plans, and a chapter containing a selection of useful resources. Each of the first six chapters contains two teaching strategies, which are particularly useful for achieving the objectives outlined in the chapter. For instance the first strategy in the book is "Discrepant Event Inquiry," which is an excellent way of introducing a unit and is thus included in the opening chapter on "Making Contact."

The book focuses on the following objectives and processes:

Making Contact. The first chapter suggests techniques for jump-starting units and lessons, by getting students to make initial contact with new material in a thoughtful way. The recommended strategies are Discrepant Event Inquiry and the popular K-W-L strategy, combined with the use of multimedia.

Substantive Conversation. In history and the social studies we often engage our students in conversations about content through lectures and through discussion. We want to make these experiences interactive and substantive for our students, and help them process and think about the content. Chapter 2 shows how two strategies, the Interactive Lecture, and the use of Response Groups, can help achieve these objectives.

Writing is Thinking. As social studies teachers we understand the importance of getting students to write not only in order to help them become better writers, but to help them think their way through the curriculum. The writing strategies described in Chapter 3 are the Video Viewing Guide and the RAFT Paper.

Finding Meaning through Reading. Whether our social studies and history readings are primary sources, textbooks, newspapers, magazines or Internet pages, we want students to discover and construct meaning in what they read. Chapter 4 shows how the Anticipation Guide and Double Entry Notetaking can help achieve these goals.

Embracing Big Ideas. We want our students to learn and think with big ideas, generalizations, and concepts. Two strategies for doing this, Philosophical Chairs and the Conceptual Continuum, are explained in Chapter 5.

Producing through Projects: Whether projects come at the end of a unit or occur earlier, the right project strategy will help students achieve more profound understandings of history. The two strategies presented in Chapter 6 are the I-Search Essay and Cooperative Group Investigation.

Chapter 7 offers four in-depth lesson plans, whose subjects are the discovery of the Iceman; the ancient antecedents of American government; the clash between British troops and colonists at Lexington Green in 1775; and the clash between fundamentalism and modernism evidenced in the Scopes Monkey trial of 1925.

Chapter 8 lists useful books, articles, and websites for the reader who wants to delve deeper into any of the strategies described here, or to search for other teaching methods.

These teaching strategies are most appropriate for middle and high school classrooms, but they can also be adapted for use at the upper elementary levels. We hope that readers will be flexible and creative with the strategies, modifying them when necessary to fit a particular topic, grade level or group of students. Although the strategies are useful for achieving the purposes of the chapter in which they are presented, many of them can also be used for other purposes as well.

The strategies in this book can help teachers to create a rich, diverse and engaged classroom environment, but they are worth little if the teacher does not possess strong content knowledge. Teachers cannot construct profound and stimulating lessons if they know little more than the students (or, as the old saying goes, are only one chapter ahead of their students). A deep knowledge by the teacher of the subject matter is essential if students are to develop a profound—rather than a superficial—knowledge of history.

To achieve the goals we have set for them, students must develop their critical thinking skills. This includes learning how to evaluate information, investigate biases, question and weigh evidence, compare and contrast factors, identify motivations and challenge assumptions. It is the goal of this book to assist teachers interested in developing these skills among students by outlining tried and tested methods that interest and challenge students.

Acknowledgments

There are many educators, including my co-authors, Geoffrey Scheurman and Keith Reynolds, whom I would like to acknowledge for their special importance in my journey as a social studies teacher.

Over the years, I have read the works of the following educators, attended their seminars, and adapted their ideas and strategies for use in my classroom. Many of their works can be found in the resource section.

BURT BOWER AND JIM LOBDELL. Burt and Jim are the creators and developers of the *History Alive!* teaching strategies and units. I have used and adapted many of their strategies and lessons over the years and can testify that Burt and Jim have made a vital contribution to history education.

ROGER AND DAVID JOHNSON, SPENCER KAGAN, ROBERT SLAVIN, AND ELIZABETH COHEN are, in my opinion, the most important names in the study and the teaching of the various cooperative learning principles and strategies. Cooperative learning has been at the heart of my teaching for years, and for this I owe these fine educators a debt of gratitude.

BRUCE JOYCE. Bruce is the main author of the seminal *Models of Teaching* and a researcher and staff developer. It was an early volume of his book that introduced me to the importance of research on teaching and allowed me to experience the power of teaching strategies and models.

RICHARD PAUL. A brilliant writer and thinker, Richard is the director of the Center for Critical Thinking and Moral Critique and the Foundation for Critical Thinking. His writings and seminars on helping our students become disciplined thinkers have not only helped me to become a better teacher, but have also helped me become a better thinker.

GARY NASH is known primarily among history teachers for the major role he played in developing the national history standards. As director of the National Center for History in the Schools (NCHS) at the University of California at Los Angeles, he has been a prime mover in the NCHS world and American history units that utilize primary resources in every lesson. I not only use ideas from many of these units, but also have learned much about the use of primary sources in lessons from them.

WILLIAM AND JEAN BRUCE have done wonderful work to bring the discrepant event inquiry strategy to social studies teachers. Their book, *Teaching Social Studies through Discrepant Event Inquiries*, was a major influence as I began to use this outstanding teaching strategy.

SAM WINEBURG AND FRED NEWMAN have each produced a body of excellent scholarly work that is very applicable to the teaching of social studies and history. Dr. Newman's work on "authentic instruction" has been a strong influence on my teaching, and Dr. Wineburg's research on historical thinking is not only important but, as far as I can tell, unique in the world of educational research.

I would also like to acknowledge my gratitude to the following educators who have contributed to my growth of a teacher in different, but every bit as important, ways.

DR. CRAIG PAUL. Craig was an early principal of mine and was very supportive and encouraging to me as I began exploring the connections between the classroom and research on teacher effectiveness. He exemplifies the instructional leader.

DAN KOCH AND CHUCK SAMBS. Dan is my current principal at the Hudson Middle School and Chuck is the director of instructional services in the Hudson, WI school district; both are also instructional leaders in the finest sense. They have been instrumental in helping me to continue growing as well as helping me pass along what I have learned (and continue to learn) to other teachers.

MARK ITA. Mark is one of the professional development directors at the Bureau for Education and Research (BER) and his feedback and coaching have been instrumental in helping me take my teaching strategies and put them together in a seminar that I present to teachers. His suggestions for the resource book that I developed for these seminars provided a framework that I have used in this book.

I also wish to express my gratitude to my friends and colleagues at National Council for the Social Studies and the Wisconsin Council for the Social Studies for their support and suggestions.

Finally I would like to thank the thousands of students I have had over the years for enriching my life and helping me learn how I could better teach them.

APRIL 2004

CHAPTER 1

Making Contact With A New Topic

Our students are naturally curious, even though their curiosity may be well hidden. The novelty of a new subject at the point of its introduction, at the magical point of first contact, can spark a student's curiosity, overcoming the "learning inertia" that teachers often feel is working against their efforts. The moment when students first "make contact" with a new topic is a unique opportunity for the teacher to engage them in active learning. If done thoughtfully, an introductory lesson can spur students to make predictions, review prior learning, develop problem solving strategies, and ask questions. Better yet, if we can facilitate our students by using active learning strategies at the beginning of a lesson, we will have not only added to the instructional variety of our classroom, but also increased the likelihood of continued active learning later in the lesson or unit of study.

If introductions provide unique opportunities, it is equally true that they present significant challenges. The ultimate purpose of any introduction is to set the tone and prepare the way for later learning. If the introduction fails, achieving that later learning becomes more difficult.

Students frequently complain that social studies courses are boring and far removed from their daily lives. Finding ways to make the content of our courses more engaging and motivational for our students is the most effective way to overcome this "content alienation"- and it remains one of our largest and most consuming tasks as social studies teachers. Getting students "invested" by "feeling the energy" of a lesson or unit is one way to overcome some of

that alienation. Once students have made predictions regarding an outcome, attempted to formulate a hypothesis, or generated a question, they are less likely to remain uninterested or indifferent to the content of lessons that address those predictions, hypotheses, and questions. Just as our interest is more readily held by a sporting event we have wagered on, so too is our students' interest more readily held by content about which they have speculated.

Strategies that facilitate such speculation and produce such student investment at the "moment of making contact" can achieve the primary goal of an introductory lesson (which is to effectively lay the foundation for later learning), because students will remain interested in the outcome of their speculations.

Beyond tapping student curiosity and developing student investment, lesson introductions must incorporate some mechanism that makes students think about the subject before any new information is presented to them. The achievement by students of new understandings of social studies is not simply a matter of their absorbing and storing new knowledge. Rather, students combine new information with prior knowledge and "try on" the new understandings they develop through a trial-and-error process. Students' ability to access their prior knowledge and to begin thinking about the new subject are crucial to later learning. Two strategies, Discrepant Event Inquiry and Media K-W-L, will be discussed in this chapter.

A Discrepant Event

The teacher begins a lesson by telling the following story:

> In 1837, a young boy named John lived on a farm in a beautiful, mountainous, wooded area in eastern Tennessee. His family planted corn and raised animals for meat, milk and eggs. His father participated in the legislative branch of government. His mother taught English in a local school. He had four brothers and three sisters. The family appeared happy and prosperous.

> In 1839, the family moved to a treeless, dry, flat prairie, where it was barely able to raise enough food to survive. Two of John's brothers and one of his sisters died. Unable to make a living farming, his father became a member of the legislature. His mother helped publish the local newspaper. John and his family missed their beautiful home in the mountains.

After the story has been told to the students, the teacher poses the question for the students to consider: "Why did John and his family leave their beautiful home in Tennessee and take such a hard journey only to settle in a hot and barren land?"

Rather than conduct an open-ended discussion of this question, the teacher and the students engage in the strategy called Discrepant Event Inquiry. Students work, both individually and with a partner or in small groups, in order to figure out the answer to this puzzling story. Why would a happy and prosperous family make such a move? Students work to figure the story out by asking questions of the teacher that he or she can answer with a "yes" or a "no." This form of inquiry forces students to focus their questions and think through the problem.

The questioning begins.
> *Student:* Did John's dad move to get a better job?
> *Teacher:* No.
> *Student:* Why did they move?
> *Teacher:* I can't answer that; please rephrase it so I can answer it with a "yes" or a "no."
> *Student:* Did they move because of a natural disaster?
> *Teacher:* No.
> *Student:* Did they have to move?
> *Teacher:* Yes.

The questioning continues until the teacher pauses to allow students to talk in pairs or small groups. During these discussions, students should figure out what they have learned, develop further questions to ask, and hypothesize. After a short while, the teacher begins the questioning again. Questions build on questions and answers build on answers until the students begin to formulate a hypothesis. The questioning continues until it is determined that John and his family were Cherokees relocated during the "Trail of Tears".

During this Discrepant Event Inquiry, students were engaged, thinking actively, and enjoying themselves. A set has been created on which a lesson about the "Trail of Tears" can unfold.

Contact Strategy 1: Discrepant Event Inquiry

Description: Students are presented with a puzzling, paradoxical, or discrepant event or story at the beginning of a lesson. Students ask questions, pose hypotheses, analyze and synthesize information, and draw tentative conclusions while attempting to find an answer to the puzzle.

Purpose: To engage students in hypothesizing and working together to solve a puzzle; to serve as a strategy for higher-order thinking and investing students in the content to come.

Application: This strategy is used in order to motivate students to begin thinking about a new theme, idea, or concept that the teacher will deal with in the new lesson.

Overview

Discrepant Event Inquiry is a teaching strategy built around intellectual confrontation. Students are presented with a puzzling description, paradoxical statement, or discrepant story that they attempt to figure out. Students then form, test, and evaluate hypotheses by asking the teacher questions that must be answerable with either a "yes" or a "no." As they move through the inquiry, students are creating questions, analyzing ideas, making predictions, and deepening their investment in the material being presented. Additionally, students gain practice thinking critically as they generate and evaluate questions and answers. Perhaps most importantly, at some point in the inquiry, students will search their own knowledge, recalling whatever they might already know about the subject, in hopes of finding clues to solve the puzzle. In other words, during this kind of inquiry, students naturally access their own prior knowledge for the teacher to build upon later.

Topics for inquiry are rife in history—events with unexpected outcomes, people who exhibit surprising characteristics, statements with paradoxical twists— anything with an element of mystery might be used for the story. The only two prerequisites are that the mystery has an unexpected outcome and that the puzzle is eventually "discoverable" through student questioning.

Procedures

There are four basic steps to Discrepant Event Inquiry: (1) Develop and Present the Inquiry, (2) Students Question the Teacher, (3) Organize and Review Information, and (4) Formulate and Present an Answer. Let's discuss each of these in turn.

1. Develop and Present the Inquiry

The teacher must generate a story or puzzle for the inquiry. Importantly, the instructor must also identify what component is to be omitted for students to discover.

It is this omitted component which, simply through its absence, creates the story's mystery. Stories that are long or short, humorous or serious, and anything a bit out of the ordinary—all of these are grist for the inquiry mill. Once developed, the instructor must present the puzzle and the inquiry's guiding question to the students.

Following the story or puzzling statement, a guiding question is given in order to guide the students in their questioning. The success of the inquiry exercise depends greatly on the quality of its guiding question. It must be answerable by the students, given the story and probable questions they will generate. Most importantly, it must guide the students' thinking toward important ideas or concepts that the lesson will cover.

Example: A teacher begins a lesson on the geography of a region with the with the following puzzling story:

> In 1000 CE, the Netherlands, located in northern Europe, had 8,380 square miles of land. The people of the Netherlands farmed 5,866 square miles. Today the Netherlands has 13,967 square miles of land, and they now farm 9,776 square miles. The national boundaries of the Netherlands are the same as in 1000.

The teacher would then pose this question: How is it possible that the people of the Netherlands expanded their land base without changing their borders? The answer students try to uncover is that at the beginning of the eleventh century, the people of the Netherlands began building dikes and dams to expel the seawater. They pumped water from marshy lands that were mostly under water, but within the nation's boundaries.

Example: In a unit on Ancient Egypt, rather than use a longer story, a teacher could begin a lesson with the following short paradoxical statement. Realizing that the tomb of King Tut was found intact and unspoiled only because it remained hidden by the rubble of another tomb, the teacher develops and presents the following statement: "This person never would have been found, if this person had not been so hard to find."

The teacher would then pose the following questions: "Who was this person, and how is it possible that this person was found only because he or she was 'so hard to find?'"

2. Students Question the Teacher

To solve the inquiry puzzle, students must gain additional information. They "collect" their data for this by asking the teacher questions. However, the questions must be very specifically structured. The instructor explains that she or he will only take questions answerable with a "yes" or a "no." The purpose is to place the burden of forming and testing the hypotheses entirely upon the students. When students are not able to ask open-ended questions, they cannot rely on the teacher to give them essential information. In the absence of such clues from the teacher, the students must form a hypothesis, generate questions to test it, and then refine their hypothesis according to the answers given.

As part of the directions, the teacher should make clear that appropriate questions are those that help one to "infer" an answer, not just questions that turn this into a guessing game. Thus, "was this person male?" is an acceptable question, whereas just guessing one name after another is not acceptable, at least not until enough questioning has occurred that the student can provide a justification for this answer. Tell students to tell you if they are about to offer a "final guess" to the riddle so you, as teacher, can control the process.

3. Organize and Review Information

Periodically, the instructor should pause, and teacher and students should organize or review key information already "discovered." It is also helpful to have students process their ideas in small groups so that they can state their ideas and hypotheses, discuss explicitly how they developed them, review what questions supported or refuted their ideas, and consider the implications of new information. Pausing to review and organize is especially important in classrooms with a wide spectrum of student abilities. The

pause for discussion also offers a chance for all students to understand not only the current status of the inquiry but also, more importantly, how that point was reached.

4. Formulate and Present an Answer

At some point a student or students will arrive at what they believe is the best answer and will want to offer it to the class. As in step 3, the instructor should pause and have students state their answer and then, before indicating the correctness of the answer, require the students to present the train of thought that produced the answer.

Discussion

As middle and secondary school teachers, we have four to six classes a day. When we use the discrepant event inquiry strategy, how can we prevent students in one class from telling students in another class what the probable answer is?

One effective way to deal with this problem is to "time" the classes and make it a competition. The time that it takes each class from when students begin asking questions to when the probable answer is given and explained is the time for the class. A digital overhead timer, or even a simple stopwatch, can be used for keeping time, but be certain to pause the clock when you are having the whole class or small groups process their ideas, and then start it again when the questioning begins.[1]

Once the answer is revealed, the teacher can review some of the student questions that led to the solution. This not only provides a motivational way to provide reinforcement to individual students, it provides a forum for the teacher to make student assumptions and misconceptions explicit before moving on to deeper explorations of the content (for example, a unit on the Pharaohs in ancient Egypt).[2]

Contact Strategy 2: Media K-W-L

Description: This strategy uses a slide, video clip, audiotape or other form of media. Students discuss and list what they **K**now (or believe that they know) about the subject to be studied; what they **W**ant to know; and, at the completion of the lesson, what they **L**earned.

Purpose: To immediately capture students' attention with a visual image, to initiate student thinking and tap their prior knowledge, and to directly involve students in their own learning by having them preview and then review their own knowledge of a topic.

Application: The strategy can be used at the beginning of a lesson when the teacher wants students to begin thinking and forming questions about a new lesson. It can also be used during a lecture (see Chapter 2). The L (Learned) part of the Media K-W-L strategy occurs at the end of a lesson or lecture.

Overview

The K-W-L strategy is a well-known active teaching strategy involving three overlapping events. Students brainstorm what they already know about an identified subject, formulate questions about what they would like to learn and, eventually, write about what they have learned. Although K-W-L comes in different forms, all versions involve students predicting and identifying what they would like to learn, which helps students develop a sense of investment and ownership of the future content of the lesson.

Unfortunately, many students respond to the "what do you know about..." by saying "nothing." Their response to "What do you want to know about..." may also be "nothing." Something more is needed to add an additional spark that piques student curiosity.

We have adapted the classic K-W-L model so that it might better serve as an active learning introductory strategy. We focus on the initial "K" and "W" components of the model and add a visual media image. A brief, catching, visual image not only serves to grab attention; it can focus that attention on the content. Additionally, while a picture may be worth a thousand words, any single visual image may raise as many questions as it answers--again creating a degree of puzzlement and offering an avenue for student questions and predictions.

Aided by teacher questions or directions, students view an image, list what they think they already know about the subject represented, and discuss their observations. After the discussion, students will formulate and discuss questions they would like to have answered about the subject in future lessons.

Procedures

There are three steps to the Media K-W-L strategy: (1) Select and Display a Powerful Visual Image, (2) Students View the Image, then List and Discuss What They Know, and (3) Students Ask Questions.

1. Select and Display a Powerful Visual Image

The instructor selects a still photo, a slide, a video clip, a single filmstrip frame, or some other visual image that can be displayed for the entire class. The image should in some way capture and represent the content of upcoming lessons. In general, visuals with multiple components and action tend to work best. Additionally, the image should be as large as possible. A large image allows students to walk up to it and point to details. Video clips can be used, but this should be done very carefully, using only a short, relevant clip.

Example: during a unit on the Civil War, a teacher might choose to begin the lesson by telling students that they are going to watch a portion of a speech that they may know of. Students are instructed to watch the video clip and jot down what they know about the speech. The teacher then shows a twenty-second portion of a Lincoln re-enactor reciting the Gettysburg Address (C-SPAN, American Writers: A Journey through History program on Abraham Lincoln, www.americanwriters.org). Following the clip, students discuss what they think they know about the Gettysburg Address, and formulate questions about it.

2. Students View the Image, then List and Discuss What They Know

With the image displayed, the instructor must find a means by which the students can interact with the image and identify what they already know about its content. How the

The Black Death

The teacher begins a lesson on the Black Death by turning out the lights of the room and projecting a slide of a painting by Pieter Brueghel, *The Triumph of Death*, onto a wall. The projector is far enough from the wall to make the picture very large. The room becomes quiet as students stare at the large image.

Pieter Brueghel, *The Triumph of Death*, ca. 1562. Oil on panel, 117 x 162 cm. Museo del Prado, Madrid.

The teacher asks students to find three separate images from three different places in the painting and write what they see into their notebooks. Students are invited to come up to the large picture on the wall and examine it more carefully. There is a buzz throughout the class while students discuss and point out things that they see; more and more students come up to the wall for a closer look.

After a few minutes the students who are up by the picture are asked to sit down, and the teacher asks students to describe what they see.

"Skeletons killing people!" shouts out one student. "Those aren't skeletons," counters another. "They have skin on their bones but they are kinda like skeletons." "Is that dog eating a dead body?" "There are fires and the skeleton bodies are coming from the sea." "The man in the upper right is about to have his head cut off!"

After a minute of this discussion, the teacher tells them that this painting imaginatively depicts a real event and asks them what it may be. With some prodding students suggest that the topic might have been the Black Death. The teacher asks the class to list several things they know, or believe they know, about the plague. A discussion ensues in which students make a number of statements about the plague. Disagreements over those statements ensue.

Changing the focus of the brief discussion, the teacher moves by the projected slide and asks "What do you wonder about the plague, or about this painting?"

The students are engaged and ready for a lesson on the Black Death; contact has been made.

Note
A slide of *The Triumph of Death* is available in the *History Alive!* unit of study "Europe's Transition to the Modern World." Please see the Resources list in Chapter 8.

teacher accomplishes this step will vary greatly, depending on the content, student abilities, and path of subsequent lessons. In general, the students need to view the image and record in writing what they already know about the content of the image. After each student has recorded his or her own reactions, the class should discuss those reactions.

Several modifications to this general framework can help this strategy to succeed when the content is complex or very unfamiliar to students. First, the instructor should generate some guiding questions or directions that will lead students to focus on specific parts of the image—especially parts they may already be familiar with in different contexts. Guiding questions also provide a degree of structure—helping students to identify specific component items that inform the larger scene.

Example: When using a slide of the *Triumph of Death*, ask students to find three specific images from different parts of the entire scene and record what they know about those component images. In doing so, students will find specific images of death, sickness, and destruction. Commenting on these specific component images is a way to build up to a discussion of the entire scene. After students list what they see in the printing, discuss these different images. Then let them know that the *Triumph of Death* is one artist's attempt to depict the Black Death and ask them to list and discuss what they believe they know about the Black Death as well as questions that arise from the picture and the discussion.

Example: In using a slide of the photograph taken of President Lincoln at Gettysburg, a teacher could direct students to look specifically at the people in the picture. Ask students to write down their impression of what is happening. The teacher might also want to point out President Lincoln in the slide. After explaining to the students that the photograph was taken just after President Lincoln had completed the Gettysburg Address, discuss what students know about that event as well as any questions that they have.

3. Students Ask Questions

After discussing what they already know, students then need to generate questions and ideas about what they want to learn about the subject. This can be accomplished through several means. The instructor can lead an informal class discussion, listing popular suggestions on the board or overhead projector. Or a more formal approach can be used, with each student or group of students formulating and writing specific questions to be discussed in class.

Variations on a Theme: The Student "Sting"

Needless to say, methods to "make contact" with students are numerous. One variation on both the Inquiry and the K-W-L techniques involves some deception. The teacher can get students to dramatize the content under exploration. For example, to initiate a lesson dealing with the protection of freedom of expression in the U. S. Constitution, the teacher might bring attention to a newly proposed dress code for the school. Only the teacher knows the proposal is bogus. She invites reactions and questions about it prior to launching into the heart of the lesson. Of course, the counterfeit nature of the policy is revealed as the class unfolds. Or, if the topic is the constitutional guarantee of free speech and the concept of dissent, the teacher might also read a "policy" indicating new administrative requirements that will require students to give up some extra-curricular activities. A theatrical student "plant" raises objections and eventually walks out of class (but returns after a minute). Dramatic "stings" like these stimulate student questioning in the same way Inquiry does and invite an "authentic" response from students that reveals what they know and wish to find out, much like the K-W-L strategy. (The strategy of Theatrical Openings will be discussed further in Chapter 2: Conversing Substantively.)

Although it may happen too often, a lesson should not begin with "open your books to..." or "take out your notebooks." Such an opening will not focus students on the learning to come, or motivate them. The beginning of a lesson is the best time to catch students, involve them, and motivate them so that they anticipate and think about what is to come. The beginning of the lesson is the time to make contact with the student intellectually and emotionally.

Notes

1. The TeachTimer, available through www.creativelearningtools.com, is useful for this purpose, as well as for any timed lesson or test.
2. Several of the examples (Trail of Tears and Netherlands Lands) can be found in the e-book *Mindtronics* and were used by permission of the authors, William C. and Jen K. Bruce (www.wcbruce.org).

CHAPTER 2

Conversing Substantively

Discussions are conversations of learning in our social studies classrooms. If we can facilitate the kind of conversations where teachers and students are pooling their understandings and drawing insights from one another, then meaningful learning can occur. Every time we begin a discussion in our rooms, every time we throw a question out to the class, we hope it will be the beginning of just such a conversation.

A good lecture delivers content in a language that students can relate to, contains a large amount of information, and engages students with questioning and processing strategies. To be truly effective, a lecture must not only present the material correctly, it must do so in a manner that facilitates the processing of that material. Our lectures must facilitate digestion of the material, not just the simple ingestion of information. Potential problems with lectures include boredom and student passivity, which can lead to very little, if any, learning.

The key to an effective lecture is keeping students actively involved in the presentation by finding ways to tap into and utilize components of the learning process itself. By doing so, we can transform our teacher-centered lecture presentations into interactive learning opportunities. Unfortunately, discussions in the history classroom have traditionally been plagued with a number of problems. All too often, they act as a wedge dividing the class between motivated volunteers raising their hands and spectators tuning out of the process. Despite our best intentions to create a meaningful give and take, far too many discussions are little more than a series of short answer or recall questions that provoke little deep thinking and little participation. The problems associated with discussion and lectures are not insurmountable. The strategies in this chapter, Interactive Lecture and Response Groups, can help turn lectures and discussions into substantive conversation.

Discussion Strategy 1: Interactive Lecture

Description: A lecture that utilizes a variety of processing strategies and different forms of media in order to involve students in the content being presented.

Purpose: To synthesize, summarize, and deliver information to students while keeping them actively thinking, reflecting, and processing.

Application: Interactive lecture strategies are used to directly teach information in a manner that has students interacting about and processing that information as it is being presented. The lecture strategies might also be inserted as a transition between activities or as a somewhat more teacher-directed activity that culminates a series of student-centered undertakings.

Overview

The Interactive Lecture focuses on three elements of the learning process to transform an informational presentation into active learning. (1) Introductions tap into curiosity and enhance student attention. (2) Discussion and processing allow students to pause, review, and formulate questions throughout the presentation. (3) Closure happens when, at the end of a presentation, students summarize, review, and reinforce new material that they have learned. Inviting students to identify unifying concepts and ideas at the end of a lecture enhances the possibility that they will develop a skeleton on which the facts and figures of a lecture can attach themselves.

A number of mini-strategies—listed as (a) through (l)—can make the lecture a more interactive and engaging activity for students. Also included below are examples of mini-strategies grouped according to the aspect of the learning process to which they are related. By selecting one or more strategies from each group, your lectures can be transformed into interactive events.

Procedure

1. Introductions

These activities harness students' natural curiosity and tap into their prior learning. Madeline Hunter referred to an "anticipatory set" as a sound method to use in initiating a

---

Classroom Snapshot

Wondering about the Great Depression

An American history teacher is about to give a lecture on the importance of the administration of President Franklin Roosevelt in the 20th century. The lesson begins with a slide of people in a soup line, followed by class discussion of that slide (see the Media K-W-L strategy in chapter 1), which includes students' questions.

As the lecture begins, the teacher asks the students to think about, and then discuss, what they know, or believe they know, about the Great Depression. Using ideas generated during this discussion, the teacher describes the first term of the Roosevelt presidency. At several points during the lecture, the teacher stops and asks students to process the information that they are learning with questions and discussions. Students are also frequently asked to generate their own questions to pose and discuss during the lecture. Some of the questioning/discussion sessions are held in small groups and some are class discussions. The teacher uses several different discussion methods to get students airing their questions and ideas. During the entire lecture students take notes, writing responses and questions in their notebooks.

During the lecture a video clip showing a portion of an FDR speech is also shown, written about, and discussed. They also spend time reading and discussing a quotation by FDR.

During the last ten minutes of the period, the teacher presents two writing prompts for the students to complete. The first begins with the sentence stem "I learned..." while the second begins with "I still wonder why..." The class concludes with the students and the teacher discussing the "I learned" and "I still wonder why..." statements.

lesson. The purpose of such a set is to focus the students' attention and thought on the lesson to come. The teacher's goal should be to engage students at the beginning of the lecture by immersing them in what the lecture will deal with. The teacher also should tap into students' prior knowledge. The two excellent introductory strategies discussed in Chapter 1, Discrepant Event Inquiry and Media K-W-L, can be applied in an Interactive Lecture. Several other beginning strategies that will be discussed in this section include (a) Sentence Synthesis, (b) Surprise Relevancy Writing, (c) Provocative Theatrical Openings, and (d) Timed-Pair-Share.

(a) Sentence Synthesis: This is a quick-write strategy that requires individual students to construct meaningful sentences from three or four key words in a lesson. These sentences are then shared with the class. The purpose is to have students actively review the concepts, ideas and events of a previous lesson through a written exercise that requires them to think about and synthesize what they have learned. This activity provides an ideal means of reviewing and refreshing previously learned material and can be used to segue into the body of the lecture.

Steps: The teacher begins by selecting three or four words that somehow capture the main ideas of a lesson. Most importantly, the words should be able to work together in a sentence. These words should be written on the board, overhead, or otherwise displayed for the entire class.

Students then share their sentences with the class. The instructor encourages class discussion and builds on the ideas being developed, if necessary. After a short discussion, the teacher begins to tie the ideas to the topic of the lecture to come.

Example: The teacher has just finished a lesson about differing views on the purpose of the Civil War and begins with a sentence synthesis of the words "President," "divided," and "Gettysburg." The students write their sentences and then share them. This is followed as a set for a lecture on Gettysburg.

Example: Prior to a lecture on the government of the Roman Republic, the teacher leads a class discussion on the United States government. The next day the students come into class to find the words "government," "Constitution," and "separation" written on the board. The teacher asks them to write a meaningful sentence with those three terms (they can be in any order in the sentence).

(b) Relevancy Writing: In this mini-strategy, students generate the "main theme" of a lecture they have not heard yet. To do this, think of one way that the material to be presented relates to your students' lives. Then, formulate a question that will require students to generate ideas that will in turn reflect the main theme of your lecture. Ask students to write down their ideas. Select the ideas of a few students for planning your lecture. Obviously, finding the relevancy is the most important and difficult aspect of this strategy. However, it is also important to return to the students' answers during the lecture and make explicit for the students the similarities between their answers and what happened historically.

Example: For a lecture on the 1920s stressing the desire of society to have fun and forget the horrors of war, ask students to imagine their ideal plans for the summer after they graduate from high school. Then, when discussing the invention of jazz, the evolution of popular entertainment, or the retreat from serious social issues in the 1920s, remind students of their own "desires" to have fun and celebrate after graduation.

If the lecture is to focus on changes in society wrought by some invention, ask students to imagine they have just invented the Internet and instruct them to write a brief letter to their parents about the importance of their invention and how it might change things. Then, as you discuss the wide impact of the telegraph or steam engine, remind students how much the Internet has changed our lives beyond simply making computing different.

(c) Provocative Theatrical Openings: Another way to create an intellectual context (for information to follow in a lecture), is to invent some kind of "sting" for the class, as briefly described in Chapter 1. The teacher must exercise discretion and prudence, of course, to insure that students' feelings are not hurt and that no one is unnecessarily embarrassed. Within limits, however, a teacher can "set up students" with a scenario that becomes a thread which ties together the rest of the presentation.

Example: Prior to a presentation on the guarantees and limitations of religious expression in schools as expressed in the First Amendment, the teacher might ask students to begin class with "a moment of silent meditation or voluntary prayer" in honor of a local or national event. A "confederate" student—contacted and "prepared" before class—stands up and refuses to participate. The tension created during the ensuing choreographed dynamics ensue is gradually revealed to have been theater as the discussion on the Constitution proceeds.

Example: At the beginning of a presentation on Fascism in Nazi Germany, the teacher marches into the room, visibly upset, and demands that students start class by writing a paragraph on "the last time you knowingly and willingly disobeyed someone in a position of authority over you." Then, as the lecture unfolds, the teacher can refer to students' personal experiences with doing things that are morally wrong (but "required" by someone else) or refusing to do things that are morally right (but unfashionable or damaging to one's reputation).

Example: Prior to a lesson dealing with Gutenberg's printing press (and other Renaissance innovations), the teacher instructs the class to copy a page from their book word by word (interrupt the task after a minute or so).

(d) Timed-Pair-Share: This is a pair discussion strategy in which each student has a specified amount of time to explain his or her ideas to another. After the teacher asks an open-ended question, students pair up. Each student has a set period of time (one minute or so) to explain his or her ideas to the other student. When the minute is up, the other student has one minute to explain his or her answer. The digital overhead timer mentioned in the last chapter is an excellent resource to use with this strategy (www. creativelearningtools.com).

Example: The teacher is about to lecture on the Athenian form of democracy. The prior lesson covered Cleisthenes and the Athenian revolution in depth. As the new lecture begins, students pair up. The teacher instructs everyone to think about describing the Athenian revolution and the government that followed. After allowing students three or four minutes to jot down ideas, the teacher tells the class that each student has one minute to explain his or her ideas to his or her partner (and vice versa, for a conversation lasting two minutes).

Example: Prior to a lecture on the making of the U. S. Constitution, students are asked to think about the previous lesson on the Articles of Confederation. Students then pair up. Each has one minute to explain to his or her partner what he or she knows about the creation of the Articles and the reasons for their failure.

2. Discussion and Processing

Allow students to review, formulate questions about, and digest the information that is being shared during the lecture. A good hook will grab their attention, but keeping them actively engaged with the material throughout the presentation is another matter. The strategies below are designed to facilitate the processes necessary to make meanings from new material. Students need to review, generate questions, and, sometimes, simply enjoy a dramatic pause to reflect and let things sink in. Several discussion and processing strategies that will be discussed in this section include (e) Question-All Write, (f) Think-Pair-Share, (g) Numbered Heads Together, (h) Whip Around, (i) Primary

Source Discussion:, and (j) Showing Video or Slides.

(e) Question-All Write: During the lecture, the teacher poses a question for students to ponder. The teacher then pauses to allow students to consider it and to write down an answer in their notebooks. Although asking for a simple summary of information given in the lecture can be effective, the best questions are those that require students to apply given information to a new set of circumstances. It is crucial to let the students have enough wait time to formulate their answers. The teacher then chooses some method for students to share responses. As they share, the teacher reinforces key concepts and foreshadows coming content. The Question-All Write strategy improves retention of material covered and increases the probability that students will pay attention and think about information yet to come.

(f) Think-Pair-Share: This cooperative learning strategy utilizes wait time, pair discussions, and whole group discussion. The teacher asks a question relevant to the information in the lecture and pauses a few seconds to allow for thinking time. The question should be open-ended, thus having a number of possible answers. Students then pair up to discuss their thoughts about the question. Following the paired discussion, the teacher calls upon a few students to share their answers, one person at a time. If any student is unprepared, he or she can count on being called the next time.

(g) Numbered Heads Together: In this strategy, students count off in their groups. The teacher poses an open-ended question and asks groups to discuss the question. Following discussion time, the teacher calls out a number. All students with that number stand and summarize their group's ideas.

(h) Whip Around: Following the Question-All Write or Think-Pair-Share, the teacher selects a method for the students to share their answers. An excellent strategy for initiating a discussion is the "Whip Around" in which the teacher selects an area of the room, and everyone in that area reads his or her answer.

This strategy can be used with a selected section of the class and supplemented by calling on individuals from other parts of the room. It is important that the question asked should draw a variety of responses. The teacher might say to the class (after using a Question-All Write), "Look over your written responses to the question. Let's whip down this row and across the back. Please read your responses. I will also call on a few others."

The "whip around" builds upon the wait time of the previous two strategies, and also raises the interest level of the class. Students often listen more closely to responses in order to compare those responses to their own.

(i) Primary Source Discussion: The history teacher can utilize time during the lecture to introduce a primary source to the students and discuss the meaning of that source. A copy of the primary source could be handed out to students, put on the overhead, or if it is an audio/video recording, played. If the students are seated in groups, give them some time to react to the primary source in those groups before initiating a class discussion. The teacher may ask the whole class to consider a political cartoon, analyze a photograph, or read excerpts from a couple of speeches.

(j) Showing Video or Slides: These resources can powerfully augment lectures. Visual images can be selected that illustrate major points, events or ideas being discussed in the lecture. This can be followed by questions posed by the teacher.

If a video segment is selected for use, it should be short (no more than 10 or 15 minutes) and should be preceded with an explanation of what students should watch for. (The video viewing guide is an excellent note-taking strategy to use with video clips. See Chapter 3 for an explanation of this strategy.)

Slides can also be an excellent form of media to use in a lecture. If the slide projector and the screen are at the furthest opposing points in the room, the image will be very large, and students can interact with what they see. This interaction can include students moving toward the screen for a closer examination, pointing out what they see, or even "stepping into the image" to role play.

Example: A teacher lecturing on the loss and rediscovery of the Egyptian language passes around a scale replica of the Rosetta Stone. After students have examined and discussed the replica, the teacher continues by bringing in student's questions and observations into the lecture.

Example: During a lecture on the costs of the Civil War, the teacher plays the recording of the Sullivan Ballou letter from the soundtrack of Ken Burns' *Civil War* video series.

Example: During a lecture on the principles of the United States Constitution, the teacher passes out a sheet containing a picture of James Madison and a quote on the "very definition of tyranny" from *The Federalist Papers,* Number 47. After students have read it, and restated their interpretation of its meaning in their notebooks, the teacher puts the quote on the overhead before continuing with an analysis of it.

3. Closure

When students summarize and review material in the lecture, it reinforces learning. Too often, lectures end with the teacher merely re-stating what has already been said or asking a routine question such as: "Any questions?" Unfortunately, this misses a prime learning opportunity. When students themselves are allowed to formulate the summaries, review the material, and reinforce their learning, that learning is more likely to stay with them. These strategies are not separate activities to reinforce or assess student learning after a lecture but, rather, components of the lecture itself. They include (k) Outcome Sentences, and (l) Media Summary.

(k) Outcome Sentences: Students think about a prompt and then respond to it in writing similar to the Question-All Write. Unlike that strategy, however, the prompt is a sentence stem rather than a question. The stem typically comes at a transition point in a lecture, before class ends or prior to moving on to another learning experience. The sentence stem might be "I learned that...," or "I still wonder why...?" A few minutes of discussion follow the writing exercise. The purpose is to get all students to reflect on the lecture and on their learning. The teacher should take some time to explain how to summarize (look for main points, exclude details, etc.).

(l) Media Summary: Video clips, slides, and audiotapes can be excellent summary tools. By using a media clip at the end of a presentation we change the pace and sensations of the lecture and re-invigorate students at the precise time when they are most likely to be fading out. Select a clip that illustrates many of the main ideas or themes of the lecture. Then, ask students to respond to a question that will require them to generate those ideas and themes. Again, after students have generated their answers, the instructor leads a discussion in which those answers are shared.

Example: After a lecture on the Holocaust, show a video clip of Nazi troops forcing people into trucks. Ask students to describe where the troops were taking the people and for what reason.

Example: Following a lecture on Celtic bog bodies, show a short section of the video *Causeway of the Celts* (www.discoverychannel.com) and have students relate what they have seen to the material that they have heard and processed in the lecture.

Discussion Strategy 2: Response Group

Description: This classroom discussion strategy has students first work in small groups in order to understand, synthesize, and analyze information and then brings this understanding forward in a whole class discussion.

Purpose: To conduct thoughtful and in-depth small group and classroom conversations following student interaction with important resources.

Application: This strategy is to be used when the teacher wishes to have students discuss people, discoveries, concepts or events as well as interact with primary materials relevant to a particular subject.

Overview

The Response Group, developed by the Teachers' Curriculum Institute (www.teachtci.com), invites students to read, think about, and discuss source materials. The small group discussions are used to enrich content analysis and whole-class discussions. Students receive written or pictorial information (often primary source materials) and consider open-ended questions on the material. Presenters are then chosen from each group to share their group's findings. This widens the conversation and deepens the understanding. The Response Group strategy is especially well suited for such important social studies activities as discussing controversial issues, examining historical problems, understanding multiple perspectives, and analyzing primary sources.

One of the statements often heard from history teachers is, "I know that I should be using primary sources in the classroom, but how do I do so?" The Response Group strategy is well suited to the use and analysis of primary documents and sources.

Procedures

There are different ways to conduct a Response Group lesson. However, to be effective, they should follow the general pattern below.

1. Collect materials for group activity

Students can think like historians and/or social scientists by viewing, interpreting, asking questions about, and discussing primary source material. For instance, in the lesson on the Iceman (see Classroom Snapshot below), students receive several information sheets about the Iceman and about several artifacts found with him.

Students can study paintings, prints, political cartoons, or photographs and discuss them, as prompted by open-ended questions. Show the primary source material to the

---

Classroom Snapshot

A Cold Discovery

The World History class is beginning its study with the prehistory of Europe. The teacher has decided to have students examine images of artifacts, "think like archaeologists," and try to interpret those artifacts. The subject of the lesson is the discovery of the Iceman, the preserved body of a man who died in the Italian Alps over 5000 years ago. Following an introduction to the Iceman that uses the Discrepant Event Inquiry and Media K-W-L strategies (see Chapter 1), the teacher moves to the Response Group strategy. The students in the class are divided into groups of four, and each group receives a manila folder with four information sheets on the Iceman. Each information sheet has a picture of an artifact found with the Iceman, a short description of it, and the question, "What can you infer about the life and the death of the Iceman based on this artifact?" For the remainder of the period, the groups analyze and discuss the artifacts, make inferences, question each other, and propose hypotheses about the function of the four artifacts and what they might reveal about the Iceman's death. From time to time, the small groups come together for a large group discussion. By the end of the two periods given to this exercise, the students have analyzed primary sources, thought like archaeologists, and engaged in substantive conversation.

Note: This example is from a lesson in Chapter 7, Uncovering the Iceman.

---

entire class prior to the group discussions or pass out copies of it to each group.

Include interesting historical readings. For instance, if the class is discussing President Truman's decisions to use the atomic bomb in World War II, then background readings could involve the rationale for the decision as well as papers with opposing views. Or if the class is discussing what happened on Lexington Green, students could read and discuss several primary or secondary source interpretations of the event.

Historical or contemporary music can be used to relate and describe important events throughout much of history. Following the playing of the musical piece, ask students to try their hands at interpreting lyrics.

Example: The class is examining the attitudes of Northerners and Southerners towards the Civil War. The lesson will begin by looking at the Northern attitudes, and, to accomplish this, the teacher selects several sections from the speeches of Abraham Lincoln.

The teacher can present the class with three information sheets. The first should contain several sentences from Lincoln's "House Divided" speech of June 16, 1858, and from his first Inaugural Address. These give students a sense of President Lincoln's public statements prior to the war. The second information sheet should contain a portion of the message to a special session of Congress, July 4, 1861, and parts of the Emancipation Proclamation. These will demonstrate the President's attitudes during the early phases of the war. Finally, the Gettysburg Address can be presented in its entirety as the third information sheet.

2. Design questions about the source material

The development of questions for the groups to consider lays the groundwork for the subsequent discussion. The questions, which guide the investigation, should be stated in an open-ended manner in order to invite discussion among the students in the group, and, later, within the entire class. The questions posed to the Response Group have two purposes. First, some questions should help "lead" students through the documents and other materials. Specific questions that require students to read all of the materials are best. Second, and more important, some questions should be open-ended in order to invite critical thinking. Students should work their way through all of the questions with their groups.

Example: In the lesson about the Iceman (see Chapter 7), the question at the end of each information sheet asked students to discuss the artifact described on that particular sheet, hypothesizing what it might tell us about the life and death of the Iceman.

Example: The information sheets on Abraham Lincoln ask students to discuss the President's changing views on the secessionist states as well as a more specific question regarding the content and meaning of the selections.

3. Groups report to the class

After the groups have had time to discuss the questions and write their answers, the whole class discussion begins. There are a number of ways to facilitate this discussion.

(a) Numbered Heads: This is a simple cooperative strategy that consists of four steps: (1) students in small groups number off, (2) the teacher asks a question, (3) students put their heads together and discuss, and (4) the teacher calls out a number and the students with that number stand to speak for their group. After several of the students have presented their groups' ideas, the whole class discussion can begin.

(b) Listen and Respond: Encourage groups, and the whole class, to respond to each others' ideas. This can be done by asking the presenters from each group to begin with "We agree/disagree with your idea because ...," or by asking presenters who have not yet spoken to consider the ideas already mentioned and respond to them.

(c) Socratic Questioning: When using such questioning, the teacher probes the explanations, opinions, and answers that students have given to other questions, and asks them to clarify their reasoning, to identify assumptions, and to draw implications. This type of questioning slows down thinking and forces students to elaborate on and to analyze their reasoning. The discussion is enriched by the use of such probing questions.

(d) Individual Response: In concluding the lesson that utilizes the Response Group strategy, students should write individually about the ideas generated in the groups and the discussion.

Students work together, but the key expectation of the teacher is the growth of each student. For this reason, the cooperative learning principle of individual accountability should be incorporated in Response Group work. An individual writing assignment or short quiz can serve as an assessment.

(e) Exit Slip: Either of the Closure activities—Outcome Sentences or Media Summary, described under Interactive Lecture strategy—can result in the use of an Exit Slip. Similarly, any Response Group may find a productive ending using this strategy. The idea of an Exit Slip is to have students do some kind of synthesizing or evaluative activity at the very end of a lesson and then show the results to the teacher on the way out of class.

Example: Following a lesson on social change during the 1920s, ask students to take a small strip of paper and fill in the following blanks with original words.

Title: The _____ Twenties:
A Passion for _____.

First Sentence: In the _____ age,
America discovered its _____.

The teacher then makes personal contact with each student as they leave class, reminding them that their homework is to complete the first paragraph in an essay that captures the essence of social change in the 1920s. (These particular words happen to be modeled after a *Time* magazine essay. Students enjoy comparing their own word choices to those of a professional essayist the next day in class.)

Sam Wineburg, in his study of how historians read historical texts as compared with how students do, notes that students are generally not able to see subtext, do not question the text, and do not make comparisons.[1] He uses the metaphor of a courtroom: the historian working through documents in the manner of a prosecuting attorney, questioning, and digging deeply. Whereas students often find authority in the text or document, the historian finds authority in the questions formulated about the document. By using Response Groups to have students read and discuss primary sources and multiple perspectives, and through the subsequent discussion, the teacher can help students question and think critically about the information.

Note
1. Sam Wineburg. *Historical Thinking and Other Unnatural Acts: Charting the Future of Teaching the Past* (Philadelphia, PA: Temple University Press, 2001).

CHAPTER 3

Thinking through Writing

Using writing strategies in our teaching not only helps students improve their understanding of social studies; it can also help them become better writers. As history teachers we emphasize historical reasoning: using evidence to make inferences and draw tentative conclusions about people, events, and concepts in history. Our writing assignments can and should be an important step in this process. Learning to write is not only an important skill that we can help our students develop; it is an important key to learning content. Writing in extended form is part of many of the strategies in this book because of its power as a teaching and learning tool.

Effective thinking demands accuracy and clarity. Learning to write out a line of reasoning is one of the best ways to improve our thinking. Writing requires that students systematize their thinking, arrange their thoughts in a progression that is accessible to others, and open their processes of reasoning to inspection, criticism, and improvement.

In this chapter, we recommend two writing strategies: the Video Viewing Guide and the RAFT paper.

Writing Strategy 1: Video Viewing Guide

Description: This strategy uses a two-column guide to help students distill, discuss, and write about the important ideas presented in a video.

Purpose: To help students learn key information from a video presentation by taking brief notes during the viewing and later elaborating on these notes by writing out answers to important questions.

Application: This strategy is to be used with a video presentation on a social studies topic.

Overview

In our social studies and history classes, we have a wide variety of excellent videos for use in our classrooms. How we utilize them will determine much of what our students learn from them. Experience tells us that our students will gain little from a video if it is turned on and run from start to finish. Even the best videos are unlikely to keep our students' attention for thirty minutes or more.

For this reason, breaking our classroom videos into sections is an important method of presentation; shorter segments are more focused on a topic and are more likely to hold students' attention. We still, however, must help our students derive the essential ideas for which we chose the video in the first place. Although we want our students to understand the main points of the video, we do not want them to be distracted from viewing it by assigning simultaneous complex tasks. Asking students to fill in answers on a worksheet while a video is playing divides their attention too much; it can be counterproductive. What we ask students to do while viewing the video is simpler than that.

The video viewing guide uses questioning, individual notetaking, written elaboration, whole class discussion, and a summarizing paragraph to structure the organization of student notes. The following seven steps are followed in this strategy: (1) Preview the Video, (2) Explain the Viewing Guide, (3) Provide a Key Question, (4) Students Jot Down Impressions While Viewing, (5) Students Write a Complete Sentence, (6) Repeat Steps 3 through 5, and (7) Students Write a Paragraph About the Main Ideas.

CLASSROOM SNAPSHOT

The Rosetta Stone

A teacher of ancient history is conducting a lesson on Ancient Egypt. This particular lesson is about the Rosetta Stone and what has been learned from it. The teacher plans to show two video segments from *Egypt: The Quest for Immortality*, in the Time/Life series *Lost Civilizations*. The topic of these sections is how the Egyptian written language of hieroglyphics was lost and how it was later deciphered through the discovery of the Rosetta Stone.

The lesson begins when the teacher shows a transparency of a two-column Video Viewing Guide, which the students have used before (See the facing page). They copy it into their notebooks, and the teacher instructs them to watch for the answer to two questions in the video segment: "How was the Egyptian language lost?" "How did we recover it?" Students jot down brief phrases regarding those questions in the left column of their viewing guide. The teacher points out that these notes will serve as "memory joggers" for students when answering the questions.

After the eight-minute segment is shown, there is a brief discussion about students' notes in the left-hand column. The teacher records some of the things that students have jotted down and, following a brief discussion, moves to the next phase of the activity. Students use their brief notes to write complete sentences about the two questions. The complete sentences go in the right-hand column, which is the "elaboration" section.

After a few minutes, students (volunteers and others) read their sentences, and a whole-class discussion takes place on the Rosetta Stone, hieroglyphics, and any new questions that students raise.

Procedures

1. Preview the Video

In the days before the lesson, while previewing the video, make note of the section that will be shown in the lesson and the display count, which is the position on the videotape as shown on the digital display of the player. (For example, the first section that the teacher wants to show to the class may run for about seven minutes at the start of the tape, from 0:04 to 7:15).

Develop questions about the topic that are answered by information on that video segment.

If two or more segments of the video will be part of the lesson, repeat this step for each segment.

2. Explain the Viewing Guide

At the start of the lesson, place the basic frame of the two-column viewing guide on an overhead projector and describe for the class how it is used (as discussed below). Ask students to copy the guide into their notebooks, filling one page with the frame.

3. Provide a Key Question

Ask a key question that will guide students' viewing and writing. Having a question to answer will help students focus on the relevant information in the video segment. In the example above, the first key question is "How was the Egyptian language lost?"

Record	Elaborate

Extend

4. Students Jot Down Impressions While Viewing

The left-hand column, labeled "Record," is a space for jotting down quick impressions while the video is playing. Tell students that neat handwriting is not important in this space. Students might jot down the following:

Record	Elaborate
Temple attacked	
zealots	
priests killed	

5. Students Write a Complete Sentence

The right-hand column, labeled "Elaborate," is for complete sentences, which are based upon the notes taken quickly in the left-hand column. Pause the video. Students examine their brief notes, discuss some of them in class, and write a complete sentence that describes what they have learned. This sentence, written on the right side of the form, should address the question that the teacher posed at the beginning of the lesson.

Record	Elaborate
Temple attacked	The language died when the last temple in Egypt where the language was spoken and written was attacked.
zealots	

6. Repeat Steps 3 through 5

If another section of the video is part of this lesson, take a moment to pose a new key question to the class and to explain that students should continue working on the new query in the same manner. (As a variation on this step, a teacher might have a series of questions on the board, and stop the film periodically as each topic is dealt with.) In the example above, the teacher shows the next section of the video, which depicts the discovery of the Rosetta Stone. A student's Viewing Guide might look like this, after steps 3 through 5 have been repeated:

Record	Elaborate
Temple attacked	The language died when the last temple in Egypt where the language was spoken and written was attacked.
zealots	
priests killed	
invading army	Years later the army of Napoleon accidentally uncovered the Rosetta Stone.
Napoleon	
demolishing wall	
Rosetta Stone	

7. Students Write a Paragraph About the Main Ideas

At this point in the lesson, students read aloud some of the sentences and discuss them briefly. Finally, in the rectangle at the bottom labeled "Extend," students write a coherent paragraph that answers the key questions posed by the teacher. To make the paragraph flow well, the sentences in the right hand column may need to be modified before being included in the final paragraph.

Record	Elaborate
Temple attacked	The language died when the last temple in Egypt where the language was spoken and written was attacked.
zealots	
priests killed	
invading army	Years later the army of Napoleon accidentally uncovered the Rosetta Stone.
Napoleon	
demolishing wall	
Rosetta Stone	

Extend

The last place where the language of the ancient Egyptians was written and spoken was a temple that was attacked. Although the language ended with the killing of the priests, years later the army of Napoleon found the Rosetta Stone. This stone contained writing in the ancient language and in Greek. Because the language of the Greeks could be read, the ancient Egyptian writings could now be translated and understood again.

Writing Strategy 2: RAFT

Description: RAFT (Role/Audience/Format/Topic) is a writing strategy that has students "entering into" the subject. RAFT calls upon each student to assume a role of a person with a particular viewpoint and to address an audience that is connected with the subject. Thus, RAFT is in a format that is different from a standard essay or report. The writing in the essay is creative, but it is not merely a fantasy. The final piece contains important information and ideas about the topic of the lesson.

Purpose: To engage students' imagination and creativity in a writing experience that moves them towards an understanding of what has been taught. The writing, though nontraditional, requires students to think about information and ideas rather than simply transfer information from their notebooks (or textbooks) to the written page.

Application: This strategy is used toward the end of a unit in order to have students write about and process what they have learned in a factual yet creative manner. The RAFT paper can be assigned as a formal paper (including notes, rough draft, peer discussions, etc.), or as a short writing exercise to provide closure for a lesson.

Overview

Writing assignments in social studies and history, as well as in other disciplines, usually take the form of traditional essays, reports, and essays on assessments. While the traditional essay is important, RAFT has a similar informational approach, but moves well beyond it with imaginative writing. The RAFT writing strategy has students imaginatively entering into the subject matter to write a creative, yet accurate, essay.

RAFT is an acronym:

- **R** stands for the role of the writer. (Who are you in this essay?) Students, with guidance from the teacher, choose a role so that they may "write themselves into an event" being studied. The students' role in a RAFT historical paper might be a participant in an historical event, a friend of a historical person, or a reporter who is an eyewitness to history in the making.
- **A** stands for the audience. (To whom are you writing?) The student chooses the audience for whom he or she is writing. Perhaps the writer will be that eyewitness reporter and the audience will be newspaper readers, or the writer might assume the role of a friend to an historical person and his or her audience may be another friend to whom he or she is writing a letter.
- **F** stands for the format of the writing. (What form will the writing take?) The role and the audience largely determine the format, which could be a dialogue, an illustrated poem, a letter, a newspaper column, etc.
- **T** stands for the topic. (What are you writing about?) The teacher usually determines the set of possible topics, which should be drawn from material in a particular lesson. However, there are times, for

example at the end of a unit, when the teacher can give students more leeway in their choice of what to write about.

Example: A sixth grade teacher has just completed a lesson on the early fur trade on the Mississippi and assigns a RAFT paper in which each student assumes the role of a Voyager carrying furs down the Mississippi to trade. Students write a diary entry for one day.

Example: A world history teacher has completed a lesson of several days on daily life in Ghana during the first century CE. As a short assignment to close the lesson, students are to write a letter to a friend, describing a typical day. Both letter writer and recipient are assumed to be living during that period.

Procedures

The advantage of the RAFT strategy is that it allows students to use their imaginations to process the information that they are learning. Students put themselves into their subject and put their creativity to work. Teachers can obtain the best results by following these procedures:

1. Analyze Key Ideas

Share some of the complexity that you want students to deal with in their writing: The topic of a RAFT paper should not be one that can be downloaded or copied, but one that students need to research and think about.

If you want students to examine multiple perspectives on an issue, it is important to have them research those multiple perspectives to understand them prior to writing the paper. Students may then choose to write dialogues between two characters of differing opinions, or perhaps an editorial that explains both. If, on the other hand, you want

A Different Writing Assignment

Near the end of the first semester, the teacher hands out a list of topics that have been covered in previous lessons. Students discuss and then choose two topics (a first and second choice) that they would be interested in pursuing further in depth. The teacher pulls students' names from a hat to determine which students get first pick of the topics. In order to avoid excessive duplication the teacher is prepared to give some of the later students their second choice, but, happily, there is no need to do so.

When class begins the next day, the teacher explains that students will write a paper on their chosen topic. As the teacher goes through the requirements for the assignment, students realize that this paper is going to be quite different from previous written assignments--they will choose the format of the paper, the "audience" that they will be writing for, and the historical persona or point of view of the "author," who is a "witness" to that event.

The teacher explains the rubric and then reads an excerpt from a paper that a student wrote the previous year about the discovery of the "Iceman," the 5000-year-old preserved body found in the Italian Alps. This student had decided to pretend to be one of the people who actually found the Iceman and write her paper in the form of a diary entry. "The Man in the Ice," the teacher reads to the students, "by Brittany." Here is an excerpt.

> The snow crunched softly beneath my boots as I climbed the mountain. The scenery around us hardly ever changed, but the view as we looked off the mountain was absolutely breathtaking. I looked to my right and saw Helmut panting with exhaustion but refusing to rest.
>
> I dropped my walking stick and told Helmut to stop. "Look!"
>
> "At what?" he said, his face twisted in utter confusion.
>
> I began hopping and jumping down a small slope toward a figure protruding from the ice.
>
> "What do you think it is?" he asked me. His voice held mild fear within its tones.
>
> "I'm not sure, it looks like a mannequin or some kind of doll."
>
> He shook his head. "What would a mannequin be doing out here in the middle of nowhere?"
>
> "Let's go find out."
>
> He followed me down and around a large overhang to where the doll lay. When we got there, though, we found the upper torso of a corpse half buried beneath the ice. Its brown leathery skin was pulled taut about its thin frame. I gasped and shuddered slightly at the grotesque figure bending forward over a pool of ice.

students to understand an important historical event that they have studied in class, the RAFT assignment would be for students to imaginatively place themselves in that event and describe it.

2. Provide an Interactive Learning Experience

As social studies and history teachers, we should never allow students to assume a role and write about events and perspectives without first working to understand them. Little would be gained from an activity of pure pretending. If the student wants to take on the role of a Voyager, he or she could perhaps learn about the Voyagers in a lesson that might view a video clip showing the reenactment of the journey of a Voyager, or participate in a discussion after viewing a slide of a piece of art showing Voyagers trading furs and listening to period music.

3. Develop a List of Possible Roles

When the first RAFT assignment is given, help students to brainstorm the possible roles they might assume. Students might portray themselves in a different time and location, as in the Voyager example above, or be another person altogether. Alternatively, students could assume the role of a participant in a historical event, a reporter on the scene, an eyewitness, a legislator, a famous person, or even more fancifully, the "voice" of an inanimate object or a "fly on the wall."

4. Decide on the Audience, the Format, and the Topic

The teacher will usually provide guidance and limited choices, but, at the same time, give students the freedom to use their imaginations. For example, an outraged colonist could write a speech to be given to other colonists, a travel agent could design a brochure for someone who wishes to travel to Egypt and see ancient sites, an immigrant at Ellis Island could write a letter to his or her parents at home while waiting in a line, or a student reporter might write an account of a coalminers' strike for a regional newspaper.

Formats could include a dialogue between two historical characters, a eulogy for a famous person or civilization, a resume, a diary entry, or a newspaper column.

5. Present the Rubric and Have Students Move Through the Writing Process

It is not realistic to expect a final written product, with well-organized and thoughtful ideas, to take shape in one sitting. Taking students through a writing process in which they understand the expectations for the final product enables them to engage in thinking and reflection on their writing. We have found planning, note taking, questioning, drafting, peer editing, and revision to be important components of this writing process. The I-Search Essay section of chapter six has a more detailed explanation of this process.

CHAPTER 4

Finding Meaning through Reading

Reading is essential to social studies and history. Textbooks, newspapers, student magazines, and primary source materials are mainstays of social studies and history classrooms.

To obtain the most meaning from their reading, students should not be merely passing their eyes over the text and trying to memorize what they can. They should be questioning, organizing, interpreting, synthesizing, and digesting what they read. The following two strategies will help students become active readers in history and social studies.

Reading Strategy 1: Anticipation Guide

Description: The Anticipation Guide is a strategy in which students forecast the major ideas of a reading passage through the use of statements that activate their thoughts and opinions.

Purpose: To activate students' prior knowledge and stimulate student interest just before a reading assignment is given.

Application: Anticipation Guides are used prior to having students read a passage from their text or other supplemental reading material (whether they are reading it in class or as homework). The Anticipation Guide can also be used as an interactive hook for any lesson, presentation, or reading.

Overview

Anticipation Guides can be used in almost any class in which new information is being provided to students. This strategy was developed originally for use prior to a reading in order to get students thinking and making predictions about what they were about to read. The guide is written in an "agree" or "disagree" or "true/false" format. It revolves around the most important concepts to be taught. Students are motivated to read (or view) closely in order to search for answers that support their thoughts and predictions. The guide activates students' prior knowledge and motivates them.

Procedures

1. Identify the major concepts in the text

Before beginning the lesson, the teacher should look for the central ideas that he or she wishes to emphasize in the passage that students will be reading.

Example: The teacher in the classroom snapshot is beginning a unit on the Black Death in Medieval Europe. Students will be reading about the causes of the epidemic. The teacher has decided to focus on the following points:

- The Black Death probably consisted of several diseases that were spread by flea bites.
- It has been estimated that 25 percent to 50 percent of Europe's population died from that epidemic.
- The Black Death contributed to the end of feudalism in the Middle Ages.

2. Identify ways in which students' beliefs will be either supported or challenged

Consider what students may already know about the topic, or may think that they know, that the reading can challenge or affirm. Do not choose facts or ideas that will be well known to students or that are not likely to provoke any discussion.

3. Create statements for the Anticipation Guide

These statements may challenge, modify, or support students' understandings. The most effective statements are those about which students may have some ideas, but not complete understanding. These statements should directly address the main points or ideas that the teacher wants to emphasize in step 1. The statements should be written to fit a "true/false" or "agree/disagree" response.

Example: In the classroom snapshot, the teacher decided to emphasize the causes of the Black Death in Europe. Some students may think that rats were the sole carrier of the disease at that time. Rat bites to humans were not the main form of transmission of these diseases—flea bites were. For example, the bubonic plague bacterium (*yersinia pestis*) would grow inside a rat. A flea would bite the rat, become infected with the bacteria (tiny one-celled organisms), and then bite a human, passing some of the bacteria along to that person. Very shortly, that person would become sick.

Some students may think that the bubonic plague was the only cause of the Black Death. Although bubonic plague may have been the main culprit, there were other diseases afoot, all of them caused by bacteria. Septicemic plague, bubonic plague, and pneumonic plague were all part of the problem. Some researchers think that anthrax was involved as well.

So was the Black Death spread mostly by rat bites? No, it was spread mostly by flea bites. Was the Black Death simply the disease that we now call the bubonic plague? No, the Black Death was probably caused by several diseases, bubonic plague among them.

4. Decide how to present the Anticipation Guide

Our preference is to begin by placing the Anticipation Guide on an overhead projector. We ask students to copy the statements down in their notebooks, fill in the "Before the Reading" column in class, do the reading as homework, fill in the "After the Reading" column at home, and be ready to discuss their work with the whole class the next

Curious about the Black Death

The teacher begins the lesson by explaining that she would like to find out what students might already know about the Black Death. Students copy the following statements from a transparency into their notebooks (making certain to include both the "Before" and "After" spaces).

Anticipation Guide

True/False Before the Reading		True/False After the Reading
_____	1. The Black Death was spread mainly by rat bites.	—
_____	2. The Black Death killed up to 15% of Europe's population.	_____
_____	3. The Black Death was simply the disease that doctors now call the Bubonic Plague.	_____
_____	4. As a disease, the Black Death was wiped out after a vaccine was developed in 1939.	_____
_____	5. The Black Death spread from Asia to Europe through trade.	_____
_____	6. The plague struck the lower classes but not the upper classes.	_____

The class is divided into pairs. Each pair of students then discusses the veracity of each statement and—making its best guess—places a "T" (for True) or "F" (for False) mark in each "Before the Reading" space. Members of the class then discuss their answers, but the teacher does not let students know whether the statements are indeed true or false. The students must discover this from a reading assignment that the teacher gives at the end of the class period. Students should return to class the next day with the "After the Reading" spaces filled in with Ts or Fs. Students should be ready to discuss what they have learned.

day. Alternatively, students could pair up and discuss their "True/False" responses, or the whole class could discuss the statements, or both. However the guide is presented, the teacher should elicit students' opinions, but be careful not to answer any questions during an initial discussion.

5. Assign the reading
Ask students to focus on the information in the reading that confirms, rejects, or elaborates upon the statements in the Anticipation Guide. Students can mark ideas that are germane to the statements in the guide. They can highlight passages or use checks in the margin to do so; or, if marking in the book is not permitted, sticky notes will do. This reading can be done in class individually or in pairs, or it can be assigned as homework.

6. Students compare students' initial and final responses
This can be done individually or in small groups. If they are working together, students can refer to specific passages in the reading when they discuss any points of disagreement.

7. The whole class discusses the final responses
The teacher guides a discussion about what people might commonly believe in contrast with new information provided in the reading.

Reading Strategy 2: Double-Entry Note Taking

Description: This strategy is a two-column note taking technique that students use while they are reading a text selection, primary source, or Internet page.

Purpose: To help students understand and remember key events, ideas, and people from a reading.

Application: This strategy is especially useful at the beginning of the year because it provides students with a note-taking system that they can use throughout the year in various disciplines.

Overview

There are obvious advantages to the use of textbooks in social studies and history classrooms. Textbooks compact and synthesize immense bodies of information. Different teachers use their textbooks in different ways: for some it is a classroom resource, for others it is the curriculum. However a teacher chooses to use a textbook, note taking can help students get meaning from the reading.

Double-entry note taking utilizes a two-column format to help students "work with" any written material. As students read through the material, they take notes in a format that provides them the structure with which to organize material.

Double-entry note taking can also help students organize the ideas that they gain from listening and viewing. As teachers, we depend upon students taking notes, yet their notes are often disorganized and lack precise information. Students may not know what to write down and what to leave out. They may copy material from a book or overhead screen verbatim, not stopping to think much about the ideas contained within. Double-entry note taking begins to address these problems.

The shape of the double-entry note guide is the same as that used in the video viewing guide.

Questions	Details

Summary

Procedures

In this type of note taking, the students' page is divided into two columns, below which is a rectangular box. What goes into the columns varies with the type of reading and the directions of the teacher as to what students should think about and organize.

1. Introduce students to double-entry note taking

Make a transparency of the double-entry format and demonstrate it by reading aloud a passage and taking some notes. When students understand the method, they can work individually, or in pairs, to practice using the form. When student are comfortable with the strategy, it can be used with a homework assignment, with in-class reading, with videos, or as a note-taking strategy to use when gathering information for written essays and research papers.

2. Label the columns and the rectangle

The headings that go above the columns depend on the lesson or reading. Let the labels be dictated by the nature of the reading and what you want the students to gain from the reading. Ideas for column headings include "causes/reactions," "vocabulary/my understanding," and "generalization/detail." Some examples would include :

(a) Main Idea—Details—Summary. This setup helps students organize main ideas and details in social studies reading materials. Using the textbook, it is easy for students to find the main ideas, which are often in bold. In this case, the left-hand column is labeled "Main Idea" and the right, "Detail." The challenge in this example is for students to restate the main ideas contained within the sections. Finally, each student writes a short summary sentence in the rectangular box at the end of the form. This summary should be kept short; perhaps one or two sentences long.

The T-Columns

On Monday, the teacher assigns homework to be completed by Friday. Although it involves the reading of a chapter in the textbook, this assignment is not to read the chapter and answer the questions at the end, but offers more of a challenge. It asks them to examine and think about what they read on a deeper level (and, for this reason, many students let out a groan).

Students are asked to divide a notebook page into a "T column" with a rectangular box for a paragraph at the bottom:

Questions	Details

Summary

As students read through the chapter, they are to tackle it one section (delineated by the large red font in their text) at a time. Upon reading a section, they are to think about and then list three or four questions that the authors of that section are seeking to answer. Students should write those questions in the left-hand column labeled "Questions." Using the written material in that section, they are to make a list of the details or concepts that answer those questions. The details that they find, however, are not to be written as full sentences, but as short phrases in the right-hand column, labeled "Details."

Finally, in the box at the bottom of the column, they are to write one or two paragraphs that they feel answer the questions posed for the section. In this case, the chapter has three sections, so students will make three "T" charts in their notebooks.

On Friday the class discusses the questions the students gleaned from the reading as well as their proposed answers.

Such summaries require active processing and provide excellent feedback to the teacher.

Students find it particularly challenging to identify the main idea in materials (such as an article provided by the teacher or an Internet page) that do not have headings in bold. In this case, students should be taught to write down details first, and then decide what the point of the section is. You should also make certain that students summarize in their double-entry notes the main messages of graphs and maps that are included in the reading material.

(b) Question—Discussion—Possible Answer. Students must generate questions from the main ideas in a written passage. This takes them further than simply finding the main point. Because the points printed in bold in many textbooks often do not translate directly to a question, students have to think more deeply in order to decide what question the section has addressed. After reading and developing the question, the students reread for details, making note of them in short bulleted points in the right column. Thus, the question is written in the left column, the details in the right, and the answer in the box at the bottom.

(c) Opinion—Proof—Summary. This setup requires students to find the arguments and assertions in a reading (noted in the left-hand column) and to support arguments with evidence (noted in the right-hand column). One sheet could contain statements both pro and con. The format also translates into a persuasive essay or statement for debate.

3. Use the form to guide and organize the reading

The double-entry note taking form is an excellent structure for use with primary source quotations. Teachers who use quotations know that they can often be difficult reading for literate adults, let alone secondary students. Reading

Lincoln's Gettysburg Address may be daunting for students, and reading the ancient Greek statesman Themistocles' decree prior to the Battle of Salamis can be positively mind-blowing.

In using this note-taking format, students work individually, or in small groups, to rephrase a quote in language that they can understand. In the left-hand column students write specific quotes from a primary source document, and in the right-hand column they put down their interpretations.

4. Restate the main point of the reading in a sentence
In the box at the bottom of the page, students summarize the primary statements in their own words.

Example: The statement below is the double-entry note taking format used to understand, from a student's perspective, the opening words of the Gettysburg Address.

Quote	Meaning
Four score and seven years ago	*A score meant 20 years, so 4 x 20 = 80, plus 7 = 87 years*
our forefathers	*The founders of our country like Thomas Jefferson and James Madison*
brought forth on this continent a new nation, conceived in liberty	*created a new government* *that would treat people equally*

Restatement
Eighty-seven years ago, our country's founding fathers created a new nation, based on liberty.

CHAPTER 5
Embracing Big Ideas

As a child, Woodrow Wilson was bored by history, later describing his early studies as "one damn fact after another." Of course, Wilson went on to become an eminent historian, but only after he learned to reach beyond the "closed catechism" of "questions already answered" (Tom Holt's terms) to the exciting themes and processes that gave those facts meaning.

This requires:

1. Posing questions that guide inquiry in the field.
2. Demonstrating the procedures that experts use to carry out this inquiry.
3. Presenting the generalizations, principles, or theories that frame the results of that process.

Adolescence is a time when a child comes into his or her full intellectual powers, making it possible for the responsive teacher to guide students toward an understanding of the big ideas at the heart of course content.

For many students, the transition from middle to high school means gaining the ability to think in "formal operations," including a newfound affinity for abstractions and the capacity to hold competing ideas in their minds at the same time. Many teenagers also begin to develop competence in logical persuasion. In short, they learn to argue and love the opportunity to exercise the privilege of doing so. Finding ways to capitalize on their penchant for argument and social discourse is therefore an effective way for teachers to engage kids in the exploration of big ideas.

Big ideas are the conceptual backbone that holds the narratives of history together. Taking time to uncover the big ideas in a lesson, unit, or course, insures that teachers do not drown students in muddled minutiae. And coming to grips with essential concepts provides the best chance that classroom learning will transfer to contexts beyond the school.

In this chapter, we present two strategies to help the skilled facilitator lead students to the core concepts and questions inherent in a lesson or unit of study.

In the first strategy, students take the real "stuff" of history (people, places, and events as revealed through secondary texts, artifacts, and primary documents) and manipulate it until underlying ideas and organizational structures appear. These ideas are then formed into mental constructions represented by anchor points on a "conceptual continuum." By holding these constructions at intellectual arms' length--through discussion and reflection--students are more likely to arrive at generalizations, principles, and rules that serve as the springboard for further learning. There is a nice byproduct of this process as well: students are more likely to remember the facts!

We also describe a discussion strategy that frequently receives positive testimonials from pre-service or in-service teachers. Borrowing from its playful ancestor, the youthful game of "musical chairs," Philosophical Chairs allows students to move about the room in a way that combines autonomy of expression with a carefully prescribed set of rules to maintain order. It involves all the students in a classroom, demands active listening, and comes in many variations, giving it nearly universal appeal.

Big Ideas Strategy 1: Conceptual Continuum

Description: The Conceptual Continuum has many variations, but the essential idea is that students are provided materials from which they must identify the "anchor points" along a single discernible dimension.

Purpose: To identify the deep unifying ideas that give meaning to facts and figures contained in course content.

When to Use this Strategy: This strategy can be used at any stage of a unit. It can introduce it and set the stage for later content; it can be used in the middle of a unit when the teacher wants students to see connections or build generalizations from among a set of facts; or it can enhance the end of the unit as a means to synthesize lots of information into a meaningful mental scheme.

Overview

A concept is a mental construction used to capture the essence of a category of objects, events, or other phenomena. The teaching of ideas and concepts requires explicit attention to structures of understanding and the use of facts to support those understandings. Although concepts abound in history, it is often more difficult to provide concrete examples for students to consider than it is in the physical or biological sciences. To help in this process, the teacher might wish to consider the nature of conceptual knowledge, as it has been described by various social studies experts (for example, Edwin Fenton)[1]:

- Conceptual knowledge includes a set of "analytical questions" that guide inquiry within a structured discipline. For example, "What conditions existed when Revolution A began and how do these compare with conditions at the time of Revolutions B and C?"
- Conceptual knowledge includes the "products" of disciplined inquiry: the theories, principles, or generalizations that one can extrapolate from content. For example, "Components a, b, and c are predictors of revolution in a society of type X."
- Conceptual knowledge includes disciplinary dispositions and procedures held or employed by experts. For example, "When studying a revolutionary event, consider the perspective and credibility of eyewitness contemporary sources, and secondary sources."

It will help students to develop their conceptual abilities if they learn to view social and historical issues through certain "lenses" or "filters." Quite often, these filters are defined by a continuum, which is in turn anchored by concepts that have special meaning to experts in a particular field. In science, an object is not merely "buoyant" or "not buoyant." Rather, it exhibits a certain degree of buoyancy under certain kinds of conditions. Similarly, one is not simply a "fundamentalist" or a "modernist." But people do exhibit degrees of these attributes in particular situations, and one is defined at least partly in reference to the other. By leading students to view concrete artifacts and events, as well as people and social phenomena, in terms of conceptual categories, we enhance their ability to discriminate the qualities and attributes reflected by people in a given context. The more we practice this mental exercise, the more we enhance students' ability to carry on substantive conversation about the content of the discipline in general.

Procedures

1. Identify essential concepts

These are the concepts that hold the facts of a unit together, including the single most important (that is, the unifying) idea. Because concepts typically have opposites, teachers can introduce students to concepts by using dichotomies. Although simple "either-or" thinking may not always capture the complexity of a concept, it usually creates a good starting point for students. Brainstorming dichotomous terms also helps the teacher discover what ideas are most essential for understanding. In the Monkey Trial example, terms that appear neutral at first ("North" and "South") become quite heavy with meaning within the context of the Scopes situation.

2. Present materials from various perspectives

Many materials include several points of view that are present in a situation, implicitly or explicitly. The teacher needs to review specific works (videos, documentaries, textbook sections, documents and photographs, or songs) to see if it is possible for students to extrapolate their conceptual ideas from them.

The Roaring Twenties

The 1920s are a treasure trove of raw materials that teenagers find exciting. The decade is filled with images of illegal drinking, legendary gangsters, heroic sports figures, changing roles for women, remarkable inventions, wonderful new musical forms, spectacular commercial ventures, and sensational trials. Lurking within this jazz age spectacle are ideological upheavals that give the images of the decade profound meaning. Following an introduction to the 1920s, including images of movie stars, sports legends, g-men, flappers, airplanes, "Model T" automobiles, and advertisements, students are invited to uncover the deep undercurrents that really define the age.

To begin, the class observes a videotape describing the social, political and economic climate of Dayton, Tennessee, in 1927. The same discovery could be made by looking at a collection of photographs, political cartoons, or other primary documents. As they watch, students are invited to jot down words or phrases that represent examples of different ideological perspectives lurking in the shadows. Anything goes during this initial encounter—people, organizations, attitudes—so long as each entry captures an "opposing force" at work in society. This video leads up to the famous Scopes "Monkey Trial." (See Chapter 7 for a detailed lesson plan about this trial.) The teacher pauses the video now and then to prime the pump, helping students identify different points of view evident in the material. For example, the class list may begin to develop along these lines:

Point of View #1	**Point of View #2**
Jazz age revolution	Traditional counter-revolution
"Progress"	"Status Quo"
North ("urban" morals)	South ("bible belt" beliefs)
Speakeasies	Baptist churches
New science (evolution)	Back to basics (creation)

This process continues, with each break in the action providing an opportunity to build on the generalization formulated in the preceding clip. Before long, students can add their own words or phrases as descriptors, summarize the ones they have collected from the video, and then add more examples as they watch. For example:

Point of View #1	**Point of View #2**
Summary: Modernism	Summary: Fundamentalism
New Item:	New Item:
Darrow (Scopes)	Bryan (Tennessee)
ACLU	Anti-Evolution League

The stage is then set for remaining activities, including the examination of primary documents or the reading of a secondary text, all building on the conflicting beliefs, dispositions, and attitudes held by different people during the 1920s. Throughout the process, students are assembling a Conceptual Continuum, providing them with knowledge that will give deeper meaning to the people, places, and events of the time.

3. Discover and define two endpoints

The goal here is to avoid a "worksheet" mindset or the mere copying of information. After students make a list of different worldviews, they still need to impose meaning on the terms they place into categories ("Why does 'North' fit in one column and 'South' in the other?"). Alternatively, a teacher might guide students to a discovery about the conceptual dimension of "conservative" and "liberal" thinking by asking students to rank a series of "letters to the editor" in terms of how much "change" each author is proposing. A teacher might also lead students to an understanding of "source credibility" by asking them to rate eyewitness or contemporary accounts as more or less credible, and why. In each case, the students must grapple with a set of conceptual criteria in their mind as the continuum is formed between two contrasting positions or "endpoints."

4. Pause for student discussion

By pausing (the video or the reading of a passage), the teacher models how students use their own thinking to complete the paired descriptors. Perhaps the video clip mentions "modernism" but does not suggest a term to explain the backlash against modernism prevalent in many Southern settings. Pause the lesson and ask students to brainstorm synonyms for the concept (for example, "progressivism") as well as to suggest any "-ism" term (real or fanciful) to describe the counter-reaction to it (for example, "conservatism"). When the teacher encourages creative ideas, even if they are not perfectly accurate, students are forced to engage in conceptual thinking. For example, a student may come up with "religious-ism" or "back-woods-ism," or something as intuitive as "anti-progress-ism." Such offerings invite conversation about student assumptions, e.g., whether fundamental religious views are somehow inferior or must by definition stand in the way of scientific "progress." By pausing and reflecting on the growing list, the teacher can see to it that students are constantly synthesizing new information into broader categories.

5. Introduce more complex content

People's opinions on public issues can be thought about as falling somewhere on a continuum between two or more opposing positions (the endpoints on a continuum). Once the endpoints are defined and the continuum is established, it becomes an advance organizer for analyzing specific statements and expressions: excerpts from speeches or editorials, political cartoons, or even conventional readings from the textbook. We like to send students home with a reading assignment, for example, where the task is to take two differently colored markers and highlight examples of the conceptual endpoints established in class. In their reading about the Scopes Trial, students encountered several interesting concepts and contextual clues that allow the teacher to introduce new vocabulary and content. For example, the reading contained the following terms which, with some deep thinking (and a process of elimination), might be paired with each other or with a new word (not found in the text or video) that the student could provide:

- Evolution, Bigotry, Tolerance, Jazz, Gospel

This is also a good time to introduce several excerpts or documents that reflect "middle-of-the-road" reactions as well as the endpoints of the continuum. For example, by contrasting a radical modernist statement, a reactionary fundamentalist one, and a "moderate" statement, students can begin to see that the dichotomy they have formed, while helpful for understanding, is still not sufficient to capture the complexity of a concept.

6. "Force the issue" by creating conceptual dichotomies

On the day following a homework assignment related to the previous paragraph, place words or phrases from the reading on scraps of paper. Students working with partners shuffle the scraps. (A series of artifacts such as editorials or cartoons can be inserted for this purpose as well, so long as they reflect varying perspectives in the debate). Partners pair up dichotomous words and prepare to defend their choices using the original text along with the knowledge they gained from the previous activity. In the Scopes lesson, students receive a historical reading with references to books, people, and more abstract ideas, all of which fit into the "viewpoints" already constructed. For example:

- Darwin's *Origin of Species* / Bryan's *Hell and the High School*
- Tolerance / Bigotry

The complexity of the conceptual dimension can be reinforced again by asking students to decide which conceptual pairs are "more or less extreme" in their opposition to one another. For example, "jazz music" and "gospel music" may reflect somewhat different points on our continuum, but they are conceptually less dichotomous than "evolution" and "creation." Or, the teacher might ask, is a fundamentalist Christian from the Bible Belt necessarily "bigoted?" Is a progressive entrepreneur in Massachusetts necessarily "tolerant?"

7. Discuss the degree of dichotomy

Once partners have lined up the conceptual pairs (while the teacher circulates and provides scaffolding for student activity), sample student thinking by picking one concept out of a hat and asking different pairs of students to answer what "opposite" term they selected. Students then explain how these words, based on their reading assignment, reflect different perspectives in the context of Dayton, Tennessee. This is a good opportunity for the teacher to integrate new content or expand on concepts without resorting to a mere transmission of information in straight lecture mode.

8. Close with a writing or performance activity

By now each student has compiled two rather lengthy lists of terms and phrases, each held together by one end of the Conceptual Continuum ("modernism/progressivism" vs. "fundamentalism/conservatism"). At a minimum, they have witnessed images on video, completed a standard reading, and engaged in discussion about relevant historical content. Most importantly, they have reviewed the content from previous lessons by using a single dichotomous scheme and have developed a deeper understanding of the context of the people and events of the period. The teacher may wish to pause at this point to reinforce and assess student understanding in any number of ways. For example:

(a) Have students come up with the most representative title for each list in their notes and then write a paragraph describing the essence of that particular worldview. Require them to use at least three additional vocabulary words or phrases from each list.

(b) Have students consider a new event from the 1920s not yet considered by the class (for example, Sacco and Vanzetti). How might someone whose beliefs are more "modern" react to news about this case? How about someone whose beliefs are more "fundamentalist?"

(c) Put students in three-person groups. Have them imagine they are in a theatre in 1925, ready to watch a Charlie Chaplin film. First, they see a brief newsreel describing a situation brewing in Dayton, Tennessee, in 1925. Have three students in each group simulate a conversation at the concession stand where one person is an animated "fundamentalist," another an outspoken "modernist," and the third an innocent eavesdropper. After this heated exchange, ask each student to reproduce the key points of the dialogue in written form and then specify the main question as well as the most salient point in each side of the argument. After this grueling intellectual work, be sure to let them watch a bit of Charlie Chaplin!

(d) Invite the class to consider a contemporary situation in which the "forces" of fundamentalism and progressivism are still highly visible. Perhaps there is a community debate about sex education or the use of school facilities for religious purposes. Or distribute editorials describing reactions to the recent controversy in Kansas over the removal of all mention of "evolution" from the state standards. The class debates the merits of this recent controversy and is later asked to identify, compare, and contrast "worldviews" today relative to their expression in the 1920s.

Examples of Conceptual Continua

Here are a few conceptual continua that can be used in different units, with a specific example for each one. With practice, you'll get good at identifying the essential ideas and anchor points in every unit you teach.

(a) Radical–Liberal–Moderate–Conservative–Reactionary

Students are provided editorials, letters to the editor, or political cartoons, and asked to invent their own continuum or to rank them in terms of the "author's views about social change." Students later create multiple names to describe different authors' views before and after the "correct" (that is, conventional) terms are applied. For a good example, a *History Alive!* unit on the 1960s has three sets of editorials, including one from each end of the political spectrum and one moderate view. The editorials comprise reactions to the following topics: Women's Liberation, Kent State, and the Black Panthers.

(b) Credible–Not Credible

Students are given accounts of an event written or described by eyewitnesses, contemporaries, and historians. After trying to determine what actually happened, they are asked to rate the documents in terms of their credibility and then justify their rating. New Social Studies Curricula such as the Amherst Project or the Public Issues Series were excellent sources of conflicting perspectives as found in primary documents (See the lesson plan "Revisiting Lexington Green" in Chapter 7.)

(c) Dissent–Civil Disobedience–Riot–Insurrection–Revolution

As students interact with textbook readings and/or lecture material concerning the prelude to the French, American, or any Revolution, they can organize events (speeches, laws, and other political activities) into categories titled "Degrees of Disagreement." Students discuss and discover the criteria for being considered "revolutionary."

(d) Alliance–Détente–Peaceful Coexistence–Cold War–War
Students are given short descriptions of landmark events in world history and asked to rank them in terms of the relationship between two countries. The "degree of cooperation" unveils itself as the events are rated (for example, in U.S.-Soviet relations immediately following World War II, there are events such as the Rosenberg trial, Marshall Plan, Berlin Crisis, and later the Bay of Pigs, Cuban Missile Crisis, Sputnik, the U-2 incident, and the Apollo-Soyuz space link).

Big Ideas Strategy 2: Philosophical Chairs

Description: Philosophical Chairs is a discussion strategy that invites different points of view about a central question or topic. The strategy earned its name because students are able to move about the room during the discussion, as they would in a game of musical chairs. A student can indicate a position on a central question or issue by moving to a different seat at any time.

Purpose: The purpose of the strategy is to encourage participation in fruitful dialogue by every member of the class while introducing students to elements in critical thinking and the tentative nature of knowledge. In addition to the pedagogical benefits of eliciting prior knowledge and/or reinforcing core concepts through debate, participation in this strategy also has motivational benefits. On the one hand, many teenagers love to "have the floor" on a controversial topic, and this strategy appeals to more assertive students. On the other hand, the rules of engagement ensure that more reticent students have opportunities to speak their mind as well.

When to Use this Strategy: Like the conceptual continuum, this strategy can be used to elicit student conceptions and generate interest at the beginning of a unit, build connections or form generalizations around a central idea in the middle of a unit, or stimulate a review and reinforcement of a central concept or question at the end of a unit.

Overview

As we demonstrated in the previous section, many concepts and ideas in social studies or history courses can be placed on a conceptual continuum. It is sometimes possible for us to define our position on a particular issue or question by considering where we would stand on the continuum. Getting students to move from simple either-or assertions toward awareness of the dynamics and limitations of "absolute" knowledge is a significant cognitive step for middle and high school students. Similarly, to see the difference between a "fact" and a "claim" (the latter being the result of reasoning, evidence, and argument) is also an important leap in intellectual development. Richard Paul distinguishes between "mere opinions" and "reasoned judgments" and suggests that "critical thinking in the strong sense" means constructing the best possible argument one can make against a cherished belief.[2] We believe that the spirit of critical thinking can be taught effectively to adolescent populations. Furthermore, placing students in argumentative situations around a big idea can serve as an advance organizer for a forthcoming unit of study.

Philosophical Chairs appeals to teenagers because it capitalizes on their nascent powers of reasoning and formal operational thinking. It also invites them to move their bodies around the classroom, an act that is symbolic of the playful and yet rigorous intellectual exercise of offering an argument from more than one position on the same issue. We first encountered Philosophical Chairs in a description by Zachary Seech.[3] The technique can be modified to serve multiple purposes in a social studies unit. We offer it here as a student-friendly way to elicit students' prior knowledge and to help both students and teacher hone in on one or more big ideas as the main focus of attention for an entire unit.

Procedures

1. Identify a debatable question

This question should be about a controversial topic with central importance to a unit of study. The success of this strategy depends on the teacher's ability to zero in on a question or topic with a natural difference of opinion in the classroom population. The question tends to work better if presented within the context of a concrete case study or an authentic artifact. Even though students are required to assume a "confederate" position at some time during the debate, the results are more genuine if different students begin with dichotomous preconceptions. In the example above, about the team name, some people will be concerned primarily about order and safety, while others will be concerned primarily about individual liberties. This helps frame the rest of the unit in terms of a "big idea," namely the classic Supreme Court "balancing test" between collective safety and freedom of expression. Subsequent content is then attached to this core conceptual idea.

2. Students ponder the question

Pause to give students time to consider arguments in their own mind. Inform them that Philosophical Chairs will provide them a chance to argue the merits of a possible injunction, and that they can indicate their opinion by where they choose to sit during an ensuing discussion. As the "Snapshot" on the next page illustrates, to sit at one

Philosophical Chairs

An eleventh grade classroom is set up with students facing one another in a horseshoe format. (The exercise will work with other grades with minor modifications.) On the overhead screen is a statement based on a case study. The teacher reads it aloud.

Jefferson Davis High School, located in a large industrial city in the South, is well integrated. A total of 550 whites and 400 blacks attend the school.

Originally, the school's athletic teams were nicknamed the "Johnny Rebs" and the school band played the Confederate anthem, "Dixie," to whip up enthusiasm at sports events. Then, in 1973, the faculty ordered changes after black students protested that the nickname and playing of "Dixie" glorified the institution of slavery. The teams became known as the "Tigers," and another song was substituted for "Dixie."

Fifty-five white students objected. They asserted that the nickname Johnny Rebs and the song "Dixie" were not intended to glorify or even to recall slavery, but were only long-standing Southern traditions. Every day these students wore Confederate flag armbands to school. They also picketed outside the gates at school sports events, standing peacefully, holding signs in favor of the nickname Johnny Rebs, and singing "Dixie."

Some of the other students—white and black—became angry at the sports events. The school faculty, concerned that fights might break out, warned that anyone wearing a Confederate armband to school or picketing at sports events would be suspended.

The 55 white protesters then brought a case seeking an injunction against being suspended for wearing their armbands or picketing.

Students' opinions about the case determine where one chooses to sit. For example, in response to the statement, "An injunction preventing the principal from suspending students should be upheld," they should choose between the following positions:

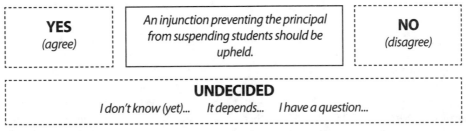

Students engage in a lively debate about the statement, occasionally getting out of their seats to relocate to another spot on the "classroom continuum." A single student moderator facilitates the discussion, which is allowed to flow freely as students move about the room, adopting different perspectives regarding the case study. The teacher is busily taking notes and only enters the arena to redirect discussion or restate rules.

extreme of a horseshoe seating arrangement indicates one's total support, while sitting at the other extreme signals one's total disagreement. One can temper the degree of opinion by shifting away from the extreme at any time and occupying a different seat. The "don't know yet" side of the room is reserved for students who see strong arguments on both sides of the issue, or who wish to pose a question to people seated on either side. Students should contemplate (and perhaps jot down) a statement for each "side" of the room before the debate begins.

3. Provide directions for the debate

It is important that everyone understands the question or issue and that a clear "either-or" alternative exists. This way, mental energies can be directed to reasons and alternatives rather than trying to identify the core conceptual question. The first time Philosophical Chairs is introduced, the teacher should provide examples of "yes" and "no" positions as well as examples of why a person might choose to sit in the "undecided" seats. While providing these explanations, the teacher should move about to different spots in the room. For example:

UPHOLD PRINCIPAL'S DECISION?

YES   Slavery is a volatile subject and, like it or not, the song "Dixie" represents something that was so offensive that we need to do something about it, even if it's a hundred years later. Let's start here.

NO   Those protesting the injunction were not the ones causing the problem. The students who didn't like their picketing are the ones creating the risk of violence. Why not suspend them?

UNSURE   I can see the concern about offending people with powerful symbols and about the threat of violence. But where do we draw the line? If we prevent this form of expression, what's next?

Depending on the class, we often require that every person speak "at least twice" and from "at least two sides of the debate" to receive participation credit. Students are instructed to raise hands before they speak and to move about the room with minimal disruption. Also, to create the "flow" of argument, one student may offer a perspective and possibly even a rebuttal or two to an opposing opinion

(at the moderator's discretion). However, two people will not be allowed to dominate the conversation. If the same person attempts to speak multiple times, the teacher may intervene and instruct the moderator to ignore anyone wishing to speak more than twice "until they are speaking from another position" or "until everyone else has spoken at least once." We like to place the following reminders on display along with the question under debate:

RULES
1.   Give short, thoughtful remarks.
2.   Stick to the issue.
3.   Everyone must speak and move about.
4.   Always present the best possible argument.
5.   Do not interrupt another speaker.

We usually hand pick a student moderator whose job is to insure that everyone gets a chance to speak. Prep this moderator to allow students to address a statement made by another person but also to be careful that the "pros," "cons," and "questions" are equally represented and that the discussion is not dominated by a few students. The moderator may also intervene with prompt statements, clarification questions, or remarks to promote an even-handed debate. Usually, we direct her to begin with a statement from the extremes, followed by a question or concern from the "undecided" side of the room, just to make sure that everyone is tuned in.

The first time this strategy is employed (especially for younger audiences), the teacher may wish to participate in the debate, providing a role model for argumentation and a willingness to suspend belief while seeking evidence upon which to form a reasoned judgment. In some situations, the teacher may even wish to serve as the moderator. However, students at all ages may surprise you with their leadership when given the chance. In fact, it is not uncommon for a discussion to go better than usual because a student is moderating. To reveal what students know, think, and believe, stay on the periphery of this activity. It can yield very interesting results. Also, within appropriate ethical boundaries, all student opinions are encouraged at first, even if they are unsupported by evidence or rigorous rhetorical devices. We like to establish equality of opportunity and a climate of openness to all ideas before guiding students toward better thinking.

4. Let the debate run its course

The teacher should resist the temptation to intervene too early. Students move freely as the debate unfolds. We encourage them to move when they hear a novel statement or an argument they are willing to entertain as a reasonable perspective, even if temporarily. While students interact, the teacher should take notes about who spoke and what they said, for acknowledgement during later debriefing. The teacher may intervene to change the focus of the debate if students begin to stray too far from the original question, if it becomes clear that class members don't have enough background to debate the topic, or if the issue fails to "polarize" students sufficiently to elicit disparate opinions. For example, in the case given above, the teacher might provoke a little more controversy by changing the prompt to one of the following statements:

- Principals do not have the right to prevent students from protesting on school grounds.
- Slavery happened a long time ago. People who still have a problem with historical symbols will just have to deal with it.

If students move too frequently or create an unhealthy distraction, the teacher may vary the logistics by having everyone remain "in place" until he (or the moderator) declares that it is time for everyone to relocate simultaneously. This may be repeated multiple times during the debate.

5. Invite the moderator to wind up

At the end of the official debate, let the moderator "weigh in" with an opinion, and give students a chance to indicate their final position on the continuum. Having "the last word" enables the student moderator to summarize what she has heard and what she feels were the most critical parts of the dialogue. The other students move to the spot on the continuum that aligns with their view at this point. The teacher clusters students into groups of three or four and asks each group to arrive at a stated position on which they could all agree. The teacher might ask: "Is there a single pivotal factor or reason that caused everyone in your group to end up in a common spot?" The teacher announces one final opportunity for speakers who have not talked more than once to get credit by representing their group. The teacher concludes with a Whip Around (Chapter 2, p. 16), reviewing key points one last time.

6. Perform a Closing Activity

There are many ways to culminate the activity. Here are a few examples:

(a) Keep a running script of the discussion, including names of speakers. This creates an opportunity to provide motivational feedback by commenting on student contributions. For example: "It was interesting when Sally turned the argument into an ethical dilemma..." or "Charlie

offered an interesting analogy I'd like us to revisit...." In this way, content can be linked to ideas arising from the students themselves. Also, many beliefs, conceptions, and questions will be relevant to other activities in the unit. By referring to notes from the earlier discussion, the teacher can personalize future discussions and ask certain students to address specific issues.

(b) The teacher may want to insert a few arguments of his own in response to points raised by students. Legitimate "arguments" by the teacher are often a profound form of praise for a teenager. Also, you may want to recall parts of the dialogue for evidence of specific reasoning strategies (for example, argument by analogy) or to point out discrete reasoning fallacies (for example, hasty generalization).

(c) Use the debate as a springboard to further study. In the case study above, for example, you might provide the "official" oral arguments presented before the United States Supreme Court in *Tinker v. Des Moines*, as well as walk students through the majority and dissenting opinions of the judges.

Limitations and Variations

We have found Philosophical Chairs to be an engaging way to involve students in the search for big ideas. Students seem to enjoy the sometimes playful, sometimes serious exchange of ideas that occurs during the discussion. Because it has a strong affective element and because the success of the discussion is based on the sharing of personal opinions (we often use "should" statements as prompts), those who are normally reticent to enter class discussions will typically share something during the activity. Although this participation is, in some cases, only for the purpose of earning "credit," such behavior is itself a phenomenon worth discussing with students. Of course, there are other limitations to the activity. Simply shooting ideas into a discussion does not insure that students will move from mere opinion to reasoned judgment about an issue. In addition, we have witnessed some students become more dogmatic and polarized in their view of an issue, rather than less, as a result of the discussion. These are concerns that need to be addressed throughout the rest of the unit. In spite of these limitations, Philosophical Chairs allows the teacher to target important conceptions or misconceptions for treatment during future lessons. The key is for the teacher to identify a topic that captures the core conceptual idea of the lesson or unit and to frame a prompt statement in such a way that it guarantees a natural split among students. The teacher may apply or modify this strategy in numerous ways. Here a few examples:

(a) Fishbowl (Use this when the class is very large).

If your class has too many students to engage them all meaningfully, you can have a subsection "take the stage" in a fishbowl format and conduct the discussion while the rest of the class listen, take notes, and later decide which "pivotal point(s)" ultimately persuaded them to adopt one perspective over another.

(b) Historical Chairs. In addition to eliciting prior knowledge and framing a unit, the Philosophical Chairs format may be useful for digging deeper into historical events already on the table. For example, using statements made by people involved in the testing of atomic weapons during and soon after World War II, students could assume the positions taken by politicians, military personnel, scientists (both pro and con), and residents who live near the test site. After analyzing opposing views, students are ready to join the debate from more than one perspective.

(c) Spontaneous Philosophical Chairs (Use when the teacher wants to analyze a specific idea on the spot). The teacher may pause to invoke this strategy by calling for a "mini-debate" at any time during a lesson. For example, pause at a key decision-making moment during a video presentation and have the students debate the pros and cons of possible decisions. A favorite example of ours occurs during the movie *1776* when John Hancock is about to break the tie on whether approval of a Declaration of Independence must be unanimous. We ask the students, "Who thinks he should vote 'yes'? Who thinks he should vote 'no'? What are the questions and implications either way?"

Notes

1. Edwin Fenton, *Teaching the New Social Studies* (New York: Holt, Rinehart and Winston, 1967).
2. Richard Paul, *Critical Thinking: What Every Person Needs to Survive in a Rapidly Changing World* (Rohnert Park, CA: Center for Critical Thinking and Moral Critique, 1990).
3. Zachary Seech, "Philosophical Chairs: A Format for Class Discussion," *Teaching Philosophy* 37 (January 1984).
4. The film *1776* was produced by Columbia Pictures, Riverside, CA in 1972. The film lasts 148 minutes.

Producing and Performing through Projects

Having students work individually or in small groups on projects is an important component of many history classes. The aim of a project is to produce a tangible product that extends and refines the knowledge students have gained in a unit of study.

There are two types of projects. We can have students simply reproduce information from a text or reference book, or we can design projects that have students do what historians do: identify interesting, relevant, and, above all, researchable questions and seek answers to those questions in an effort to explain what the past means, not just what it was.

The prevailing view of "research" among teenagers (and often among teachers) is "looking up information" and writing it down. In fact, true research is the process by which a trained expert uses the tools and procedures of a particular school of inquiry to explore real questions for which the answers are not already established. Hence, the question "What was prohibition?" albeit important, is one that does not inspire an authentic historical exploration. We can simply look up what "prohibition" was in the context of the United States of the 1920s, consulting with authoritative resources to provide us the descriptions. The question we might instead consider is: "How did prohibition influence American society in the 1920s?" This type of question allows our students to do more than merely "locate information" about the subject. They must utilize multiple sources, "interrogate" those sources, examine artifacts from the past, and focus their analytical lenses in an attempt to discover generalizable concepts and principles that are useful for understanding history, not just knowing isolated facts.

Whenever possible, we should invite our learners into the field of authentic historical research. We should guide them to recognize researchable questions and prod them to conduct explorations in search of answers to those questions. In this section, we hope to challenge the preconceptions of many students (and teachers) about "research" and "projects," and to foster higher levels of thinking about authentic historical problems.

We strongly recommend that teachers encourage students to do projects for local, state and regional history fairs, as well as for events related to National History Day.[1] Such projects enable students to enhance their skills in the use of primary sources, and can take many forms, such as research papers, exhibits, performances, or the production of documentaries.

One of the strategies in this chapter is an individual writing project, while the other is a group research/presentation project. The individual project, the I-search essay, utilizes student research, note taking, and writing to help students question history—specifically to think about, analyze, and learn historical ideas and material. The other strategy, the Cooperative Group Investigation, seeks to achieve this objective in a group setting.

Projects Strategy 1: The I-Search Essay

Description: A traditional form of essay, with thoughtfully structured and focused writing, which is the culmination of an authentic historical investigation. The I-Search Essay means "I am searching."

Purpose: To engage students in a writing experience that moves them towards thoughtful and precise writing.

Application: This strategy can be used when the teacher wishes to engage students in authentic intellectual work, culminating with a writing assignment. Students must utilize prior knowledge as well as find and synthesize new information to answer a genuine historical question.

Overview

There is an important place for the traditional essay in history teaching. An assignment to write a well-structured essay invites the students to search out information, take careful notes, consider the importance of the information that they have found, and write with precision.

Writing assignments can require students to seek out new sources, answer questions, clarify meaning, and test ideas. The I-Search essay is a research essay with an element of personal choice. Students choose a topic, search for information, analyze what they find, and express their new understanding in writing. The final essay should contain information and analysis that goes beyond the material presented in the classroom.

Procedures

1. Ask research questions

The theme of an I-Search Essay should be phrased as a question, or questions. Teachers can provide this type of focus by modeling the art of creating good questions, and then having students practice it. The teacher should spend time with students developing their ability to ask questions about a historical event or period that call for an answer that is more than a simple replication of information. On initial assignments, and in the middle grades, teachers may wish to provide topics and questions for students to research.

For example, a unit of study on the Middle Ages can be the source of many topics and questions.

CLASSROOM SNAPSHOT

The I-Search Essay

A tenth grade world history class conducts a brief survey on the Middle Ages in Europe. Using an assortment of strategies, including those based on Interactive Lectures and Response Groups (see Chapter 2), students touch on topics such as the Vikings, the Black Death, the training of knights, and the life of Joan of Arc. The teacher is careful to imply, and sometimes state explicitly, that certain questions can lead to useful further investigation. With the help of student input, these and additional questions are fleshed out and framed as research topics for students to choose from. Although the teacher exerts some control to make certain that major topics are covered, students have some choice in identifying and selecting a topic.

With models from the teacher serving as a guide, students work to dissect their topic into questions that will be answered in a final essay. With these questions in mind, students complete a preliminary writing exercise outlining the purpose of the project and final paper. The teacher explains the scoring rubric, and students then set out to locate pertinent information. The information that they gather is written in short phrases (as opposed to full sentences copied from a book) with citations (to leave a clear trace to the source of each fact or idea).

Following several class periods devoted to researching their questions, students write a first draft, then get together in pairs to read papers to each other and conduct a "pairs check." Each student uses the result of this check to begin working on his or her final draft.

FEUDALISM

- What was the relationship between the lord and vassal in the feudal system?
- What were some of the other positions in the feudal structure?
- Why did the system known as feudalism come to an end?

KNIGHTHOOD

- If you were going to be a knight in the Middle Ages, what type of training would you go through?
- Once you officially became a knight, what would your job be?
- What types of weapons and armor would you have?

CASTLES

- If you were a builder in the Middle Ages, why might you be asked to build a castle?
- What were the primary purposes of castles?
- As a builder, what type of defense would you put into the castle and why?

2. Select the topic with students

Students need to participate in the selection of their topics because this will increase their interest and motivation. The teacher must have some control over the topics, because too many students working on the same topic would invite plagiarism (not to mention the strain it would place on the resources of the media center). One possible approach is for the teacher to develop a list of topics and randomly assign each student a topic by drawing names out of a hat. Students would then have the option of suggesting an alternative topic. Our experience is that while most students will stay with the topic that they have received, some will have an interesting and original alternative topic on which they would like to work.

3. Share the rubric with students

A rubric is the set of scoring criteria that the teacher uses to evaluate students' work. It makes a great deal of sense for students to share with students the criteria by which their work will be evaluated. With a rubric in place, "misunderstandings" about the assignment are less likely to happen. Students can read what is expected of them, and can use the rubric to improve their work.

This rubric was used in the Middle Ages I-Search Essay described in the classroom snapshot and cited in the examples. The numbers represent achievement on each criterion and are not to be added up (that is, the criteria are not all of equal weight in the student's final grade for the essay).

Rubric for Individual Essay

Five paragraphs clear and done per instructions

5	4	3	2	1	O

No errors in grammar, spelling, sentence structure

5	4	3	2	1	O

High degree of clarity /excellent explanations

5	4	3	2	1	O

Questions posed are thought through/addressed

5	4	3	2	1	O

Essay shows very good research

5	4	3	2	1	O

The Pairs Check was done/suggestions followed

5	4	3	2	1	O

---

4. Talk about the process of writing

Many students do not view writing as a process, but as a final product ("I find information, copy it on a paper, and hand it in"). But writing is like thinking; we should not expect essays to suddenly emerge, full-blown and complete at the beginning. We must help students see the evolutionary nature of the process. Many models that describe the writing process refer to a series of phases such as planning, information gathering, prewriting, drafting, revising (with possible peer review), and final editing. The following organizing system (steps 5 through 10) works well in social studies classrooms. It starts with a statement of intent and a system of note-taking and continues through the process of creating drafts and revising them as a result of teacher and peer feedback and culminates with the writing of the final draft. Before leading students through steps 5 through 10, make certain that they have identified researchable questions and understand the rubric.

5. Students compose a statement of intent

In this short statement, students explain their understanding of what is expected of them in the writing assignment. Students should write the statement in their notebooks after some preliminary research, but prior to beginning the actual essay.

6. Students take notes rather than copy

Without clear directions for taking notes, students may view finding information for use in the essay as simply a process of copying sentences down. The Double-Entry

Note Taking strategy (Chapter 4) can be used effectively for taking notes for the essay. The left-hand column can be used for questions, while the right is used for bulleted notes, and the box can be used for sentence summaries that address the question at hand.

To help ensure that students are taking effective notes, whether they are using index cards or notebooks, several points should be kept in mind:

(a) Students can list their questions on separate pages and find points in their search that relate to those questions. The point is to emphasize the questions each student is trying to answer in his or her essay.

(b) Students should use short statements and bullets. The teacher can model this sort of note taking and mention the analogy of buying a classified ad in the newspaper: Every word costs you money, so keep it short! The teacher may require students to provide "end-of-the-day" summaries on how the notes they have taken address the question at hand. These summaries could go in the "summary box" at the bottom of the double-entry notes.

(c) Have students use additional shortcuts and forms of notations, such as putting a "P" for place, "E" for event, "I" for inference, or "C" for (tentative) conclusion.

7. Students start writing

When students start writing, they should begin with the middle paragraphs. Although most students want to begin with the introduction, it is usually more efficient to start with the body of the paper. For novice writers, it is easier to begin with "descriptive information." By starting with the middle paragraphs, they can immediately begin converting their notes and ideas into "evidence" in support of a tentative conclusion.

8. Students perform a Pair Check

This peer review activity has students reading and assessing each other's work-in-progress. They use a check sheet that asks students to follow certain scoring criteria when looking at each other's writing.

(a) Distribute a pair checklist with criteria that reflect those in the rubric. Middle school students use the sample checklist below when they are writing a historical essay. In this assignment, students must decide whether to ally their fictional city-state with Athens or Sparta prior to the outbreak of the Peloponnesian War. The lesson was adapted from the Teachers' Curriculum Institute's *Greek Against Greek: Athens v. Sparta.*

Pairs Check List: Athens v. Sparta Speech

___*Writer*   ___*Checker*

___ The introduction explains the purpose of the paper ___

___ The second paragraph gives at least two arguments made by each city-state ___

___ The third and fourth paragraphs lists reasons for choosing to ally with either Athens or Sparta ___

___ The final paragraph is a one- or two-sentence summary ___

___ No spelling or grammatical errors ___

___ The essay is in the form of a speech ___

Changes suggested:

(b) Pair students up, so they can provide feedback to one another. The best way to do this is a matter of debate. The teacher could pair up better writers with those who are less advanced in their writing skills. Or, the teacher could pair students who have similar abilities. We like to pair up students who are "better" writers with less-skilled ones initially, and then pair up writers of similar skill with each other secondarily.

(c) Have the students read and check each other's paper with the use of the Pairs Check List. Each student makes notes about what improvement his or her partner could make on the paper.

9. Teacher provides guidance

Depending upon the time available, conferencing with the teacher can be very helpful at this point. Students are asked to make any additional comments or ideas they get from peer reading, and turn in their rough drafts. Read through these and make comments on how students might improve their writing or clarify their thoughts. Because you are only looking through two or three paragraphs, not grading the papers, this guidance task does not take long. The next day, hand the papers back to students.

10. Students prepare a final draft

At this point, many teachers have the students work in the computer lab to write the final paper. Another option is to have students work on their final draft outside of class and give them several days to complete it. A small copy of the rubric can be stapled onto the paper. The teacher can write remarks on the rubric so that students understand exactly how they are being evaluated.

The grade that is on the final copy that is turned in need not be the "final grade" for the paper. If they so desire, students can use the rubric and remarks by the teacher to rewrite their paper and turn it in within a certain time frame. The final grade can be an average of the grades on the original and the revision, or the revised paper can account for all of the final grade. Allowing for revision permits students to consider the rubric and what they can do to improve their work.

Projects Strategy 2: Cooperative Group Investigation

Description: An activity in which students work together to investigate a research question and present their findings to the class in a creative yet informative manner.

Purpose: To allow students to pool their resources, further their own understanding, and cooperate with peers in making a formal presentation.

Application: This strategy is most effective when the teacher conducts small group work to enrich student understanding of course content.

Overview

Cooperative Group Investigation, based on Spencer Kagan's Co-op Co-op and Yael and Shlomo Sharan's Group Investigation, is a cooperative learning strategy that involves students in planning a research project, carrying it out, and then presenting it to the class.[2]

Cooperative Group Investigation is structured to maximize the opportunity for small groups of students to work together to further their own understanding of a portion of the curriculum. Eventually a group product or presentation is created and shared with the class.

This is a particularly good strategy to use when we are feeling the time crunch—too much left in the curriculum, too little time to teach it. If the teacher wishes to cover more material than there is time to do so, Cooperative Group Investigation is the strategy to use. Student cooperative groups can each take a portion of what was left, study it, and teach it to the class.

Procedures

Although there are a number of ways to approach Cooperative Group Investigation, certain steps are seen consistently across variations (figure at right).

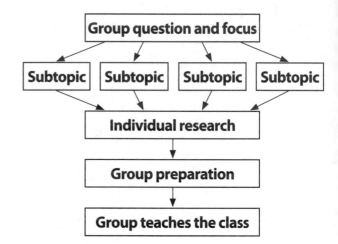

1. Hold a brief student-centered class discussion

When the teacher decides to use this strategy (whether at the beginning, middle, or end of a unit, or as a way to complete the curriculum), a class discussion is held on the project's general subject matter. The purpose of the discussion is to increase student involvement by sparking students' curiosity.

CLASSROOM SNAPSHOT

Cooperative Group Investigation

A world history teacher has only a few weeks remaining in the semester and would like to cover many of the notable scientists and inventors during the Renaissance. The unit of study begins with several introductory lessons on the Renaissance that culminate in a discussion of some European scientists and inventors. But there is too much material for the teacher alone to cover in the remaining weeks, so she lays out a plan for the whole class to participate in learning and teaching about these fascinating Renaissance men and women.

2. Select student groups and topics

Group selection should be done in the way that the teacher deems most appropriate. Depending on the teacher's preferences, the student groups may choose their topics from a previous discussion, they may be given a list from which to choose, or the topics may be assigned. As with the I-Search Essay, the topic and the focus of the subsequent group presentation should be to answer historical questions.

3. Select subtopics for research

An important principle of cooperative learning is individual accountability. When the group work is structured so that each individual is accountable for his or her work, students cannot "hitchhike" or depend on the work of others for their grade.

The subtopic selection process allows individual accountability to be structured into Cooperative Group Investigation. The group discusses its topic and divides it further into subtopics. Using the above example of ancient civilizations, one group might select Egypt, and divide the topic into subtopics such as pharaohs, mummification of the dead, the building of the pyramids, and hieroglyphics. In the example of the Renaissance inventors, individual scientists could serve as subtopics. Each student is given time to collect, analyze, and organize information relevant to his or her subtopic. Each student will also make a presentation of his or her findings to the group (and the teacher might require an individual paper).

4. Prepare and present the main topics

Following the individual presentations to the group, each cooperative learning team must then discuss the format of the team presentation. It must integrate these subtopics in a presentation that could take a variety of forms, such as panel discussions, dramatizations, learning centers, simulations, demonstrations, etc.

During the presentations, teams are told that they are in charge of teaching the class. They are responsible for how the time, space, and resources of the class are used, within limits defined by the teacher.

The scheduling and length of the Cooperative Group Investigation is up to the teacher.

Group Investigation projects are particularly useful at the end of a quarter or semester because they allow students to extend and integrate knowledge they have acquired over previous units.

5. Assess individual effort

One of the most common objections to having students work in groups is that some members will end up doing all of the work while others just "hitchhike." There are at least two ways to create individual accountability in a group activity:

a. Have each student take a quiz, complete a task (such as the subtopic preparation discussed above), or write an essay on the group product or performance;
b. Make sure each group member has a designated and separate role to perform as part of the group's report.

The Cooperative Group Investigation strategy can use both types of assessment. Even though each group member has a designated subtopic of the subject to study, there is no guarantee that he or she will follow through with the cooperative planning for the group's presentation. The teacher may wish to address this issue with an individual feedback form for each student.

In the end, feedback and evaluation should include both an individual and a group component. However, one cannot insure individual accountability if one uses group grades. Group grades not only ignore the principle of individual accountability; they are unfair to students. Thus, a group grade or component should only be a small part of an individual's final grade for the project.

Notes

1. National History Day is a year-long event (despite its title) in which students compete to present the results of their investigation of a historical question through the use of primary sources. Students may participate individually or in groups, and their project can take the form of a research paper, exhibit, performance or documentary. The National History Day finals are held at the University of Maryland, College Park, MD (the headquarters of National History Day) in June, when national winners in each project category are announced. See www.nationalhistoryday.org for more information.
2. For more details about the Kagan and Sharan strategy, see Spencer Kagan, *Cooperative Learning* (San Clemente, CA: Kagan Cooperative Learning, 1995).

Lesson Plans

The strategies discussed in this book have been used in a variety of social studies and history classrooms by the authors. This chapter contains four lessons that demonstrate a number of strategies. The lessons—Uncovering the Iceman, the Roman Antecedents of The American Constitution, What Really Happened on Lexington Green?, and Fundamentalism and Modernism in the Scopes Monkey Trial—have been developed for and used in middle school and high school history classes.

Lesson 1: Uncovering the Iceman

In this lesson, student think like archaeologists as they work with pictorial and written information on the artifacts found with the Iceman, a 5,300-year-old mummy found in the Italian Alps in 1991. Using this evidence, students in groups and as individuals, develop inferences as to whom the Iceman was and what might have happened to him, and then write a "newspaper article" on their experiences with the Iceman. Students are then introduced to what historians have learned about the Iceman's life and death.

Outcomes

The learner will

1. Develop an understanding of the archaeological find of the Iceman.
2. "Think like an archaeologist" and, given the description of various artifacts, develop a hypothesis on the life and death of the Iceman.
3. Identify and use processes important to reconstructing and reinterpreting the past and develop an understanding of how the Iceman helps historians to reconstruct life in prehistoric Europe.
4. Create a newspaper report detailing the Iceman's discovery, hypothesize as to who he was and what happened to him, and insert himself or herself as an active part of this discovery.

Teaching Strategies

* Discrepant Event Inquiry (Chapter 1)
* Media Hook/K-W-L (Chapter 1)
* Response Groups (Chapter 2)
* Video Viewing Guide (Chapter 3)
* RAFT paper (Chapter 3)

Time

The entire Iceman lesson will take about a week, but the time will vary according to the type of scheduling and whether the teacher decides to assign the RAFT paper as homework or work in class.

Resources

* One or more videos, *Iceman: Hunt for a Killer* (Discovery Communications Inc., discoverychannel. com, Bethesda, MD, 52 minutes, 2003) or
  "Patricians and Plebeians: Experiencing a Struggle for Power," in *Ancient Rome* (*History Alive!*, Teachers Curriculum Institute, www.historyalive.com).
* The following handouts are provided in the text below:
  Response Group Information Sheets (Figures 7.1 through 7.5)
  Directions for "The Iceman and Me" RAFT Paper
  Iceman Pairs Check/Rubric

Procedures

1. Anticipatory Set: Prior to the lesson divide students into groups of four. After explaining the rules of a Discrepant Event Inquiry, present the following paradoxical statement to students: "I learned more about early history from this person than anyone else. Yet this person never knew the meaning of the word 'history.'"

Allow the "yes" and "no" questioning to begin. Stop during the process in order to have groups process what they have learned from the questioning and develop new questions.

The teacher will have to decide what to accept as an answer to the inquiry. Experience with many classes demonstrates that most students are aware of the Iceman and reach this answer. However, students should be able to arrive at the understanding that the person involved belonged to the period we know as "prehistory."

2. Following the inquiry, discuss the answer that students came up with, what the clues were that helped them arrive at the answer, and what they know about the life of "prehistoric people." During this discussion, list what the students feel that they "know" about prehistoric people (if it is not brought up in the course of the discussion, mention that different prehistoric peoples adapted and evolved their ways of life according to their needs and at different rates). Include in the discussion what they know about the Iceman. Make a list of ideas about prehistoric life and the Iceman as they are brought up in class.

The previous discussion has students delving into their prior knowledge regarding prehistoric people (the "K" of KWL). During the next portion of the lesson, students will develop questions as the teacher uses the Media Hook/K-W-L strategy. A Video Viewing Guide (Chapter 3) could be distributed at this point. For the media component, the teacher plays the first few minutes of the Discovery Channel video *Iceman: Mummy from the Stone Age*. The segment begins by showing the Alps and mentions that ever so often we find scraps of evidence of early humans, but that one man left us more, "he came back." It then explains how the Iceman was found and shows footage by the people who removed the Iceman from the glacier. The teacher pauses or stops the program at "it's no unsolved murder but it is a mystery; one of the most stunning in archaeological history."

3. Following the video the teacher refers to the statement about it being a mystery. This is where the teacher segues into the W (want to know) portion of the K-W-L by inquiring about student ideas and questions. At this point display a transparency of the information sheet on the Iceman's body (Figure 7.1).

Use this transparency in order to model the upcoming Response Group activity. Read through it and discuss the possible inferences that students could make from this information. Have students jot down a few facts and questions that arise from the reading. Discussion questions include the questions that students raise as well as the following:

- What was discovered about the Iceman's body?
- What might he have been doing so high in the mountains?
- What can we infer about his life from what was found on the body?

Following the discussion, each student is to write on the open-ended question on the sheet: "What can you infer about the life and death of the Iceman from the body? Explain the reasons for your inferences." Those students who like to sketch could sketch the picture of the body in their notebook while others could describe it.

4. Pass out the Response Group artifact information sheets (the boots, the ax, the quiver, and the pouch, figures 7.2 through 7.5, respectively). Each page should be a different color in order to facilitate sorting and responding to them. Have students do a quick Roundtable to become familiar with the information (groups pass each information sheet around until every student in each group has quickly examined each one. See Chapter 2). Briefly run through the information sheets and remind groups that they are to do the same with these as the whole class did with the information sheets on the Iceman's body.

Figure 7.1

This is the Iceman. He was found up over 10,000 feet in the Italian Alps. Later study of him showed that his body had a number of compressed or broken ribs on the right side. Although scientists did not find any food in his stomach, they did find some food in the large intestines. His body contained grains of wheat and there was residue of copper in and on his hair. X-rays also showed what appeared to be a small object or bone in his back.

What can you <u>infer</u> about the life and death of the Iceman from the body? Explain the reasons for your inferences.

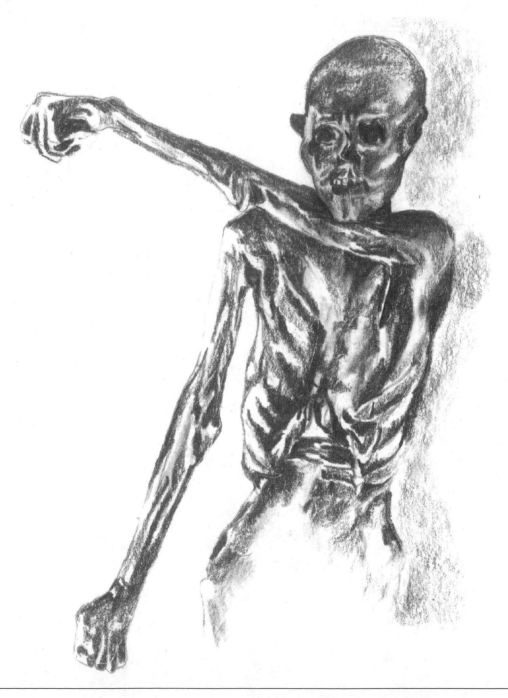

Figure 7.2.

This is a drawing of the Iceman's boots. Each boot consisted of an oval piece of leather with its edges turned up and bound with strong leather straps. The soles of the shoes were made with hide and were bound up with leather straps. Inner socks were made of knotted cord that formed nets to hold grass and weeds in place (for warmth). Grains of wheat were found on the boots.

What can you <u>infer</u> about the life and death of the Iceman from this artifact? Explain the reasons for your inferences.

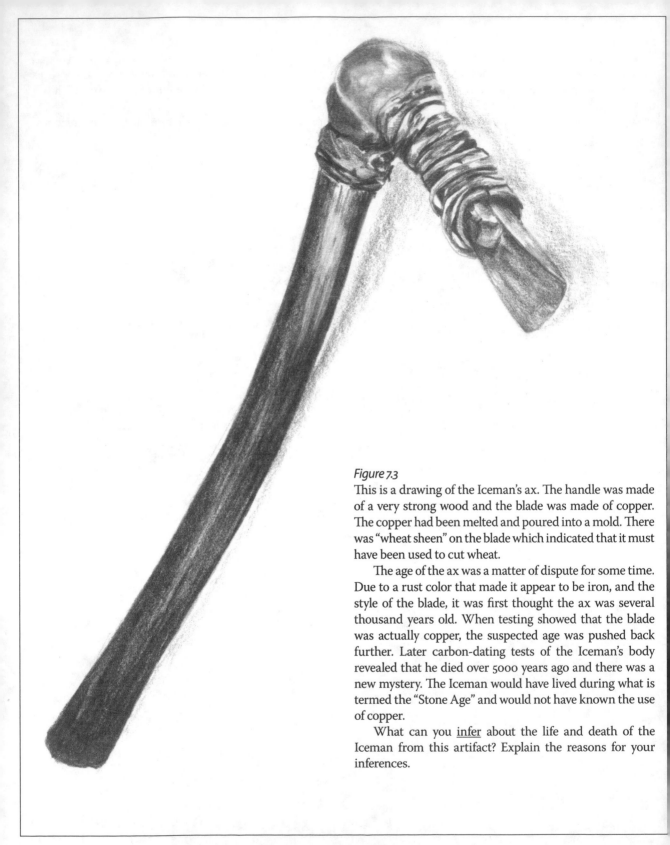

Figure 7.3

This is a drawing of the Iceman's ax. The handle was made of a very strong wood and the blade was made of copper. The copper had been melted and poured into a mold. There was "wheat sheen" on the blade which indicated that it must have been used to cut wheat.

The age of the ax was a matter of dispute for some time. Due to a rust color that made it appear to be iron, and the style of the blade, it was first thought the ax was several thousand years old. When testing showed that the blade was actually copper, the suspected age was pushed back further. Later carbon-dating tests of the Iceman's body revealed that he died over 5000 years ago and there was a new mystery. The Iceman would have lived during what is termed the "Stone Age" and would not have known the use of copper.

What can you <u>infer</u> about the life and death of the Iceman from this artifact? Explain the reasons for your inferences.

Figure 7.4

This is a drawing of the Iceman's fur quiver. Although most of the outwardly facing fur had disappeared by the time it was found, it was determined that the fur was probably that of a deer. The main part of the fur quiver was folded over and sewn together. The quiver contained fourteen arrows, but only two were finished. The supportive wood frame was broken into three pieces. The accompanying bow was not finished.

The finished arrows contained flint arrowheads, wooden shafts, and the feathers of a large brownish bird. The feathers were attached to the wood by means of birch tar and long strings made of sheep's wool.

What can you <u>infer</u> about the life and death of the Iceman from this artifact? Explain the reasons for your inferences.

Figure 7.5

This is a drawing of the pouch found near the Iceman. Archaeologists had never before found such an artifact. In the pouch were several objects including a fungus ball that contained a bacteria killing fungus, three different sized pieces of flint, and a pencil-like splinter made from goat bone. There were also several "sloe berries" found in the pouch. These berries could have made a high carbohydrate snack, but would probably not have been picked until after the first frost (due to tartness).

What can you <u>infer</u> about the life and death of the Iceman from this artifact? Explain the reasons for your inferences.

In their notebooks students can sketch the artifact pictures (or describe them) and jot down their group's observations, inferences, and the reasons for those inferences. Discuss the ideas and inferences in a whole class discussion and describe how an archaeologist or historian might attempt to link these inferences in order to create a story of who the Iceman was, and what happened to him.

5. Following the whole class discussion, explain to students that they will be putting their ideas into a fictional newspaper article, "The Iceman and Me." They are individually to attempt to create a story involving who the Iceman was and what happened to him. Read these directions aloud:

> This paper will be a factual newspaper account of the find and the story of the Iceman. There will be one bit of fiction, however: place yourself within the story somehow. You can be one of the discoverers, a news reporter, one of the scientists working on the find, or some other interested party.

Ask students to begin to create this story by specifically looking at the inferences made in the response group activity and subsequent discussion. In this RAFT Paper, students will be imagining that somehow they were involved in the finding and the subsequent study of the Iceman. In the paper, they will explain the find and their inferences as to who he was, and what happened to him.

6. Discuss the rubric for this writing assignment with the class (shown below).

7. Students can begin the writing assignment in class, but most of the researching and the writing is done as a homework assignment. Ask students to bring in a draft of the newspaper article and check it with a partner (using a Pairs Check, figure 7.6). They can make any needed revisions at home and turn in the finished article the next day.

8. Closure: In the closure for the lessons, students tie together the archaeological find of the Iceman with what has been learned about prehistoric life.

One way to do this is to show a transparency that lists some of the tentative conclusions that archaeologists have made about the Iceman (figure 7.7). Discuss how professional archaeologists arrived at these conclusions (which are always subject to revision on the basis of further findings).

Continued on p. 66

Rubric for Writing Assignment

Five Paragraphs	10	9	8	7	6	5
No grammatical errors	10	9	8	7	6	5
Introduction creatively places the student in the story and explains findings	10	9	8	7	6	5
More than two artifacts are explained and inferences made about to the Iceman's life and death (Explanation and clarity are important here)	10	9	8	7	6	5
Conclusion sums up and explains the student's theory as to who the Iceman was and what happened to him	10	9	8	7	5	6
Postscript, with newest information and student evaluation of the class	10	9	8	7	6	5

Figure 7.6

Iceman Pairs Check

Your newspaper article "The Iceman and Me" should meet each of the six criteria listed below. Check your work, then ask your partner to check it.

AUTHOR CHECK		PARTNER CHECK
_____	Five paragraphs	_____
_____	No grammatical errors	_____
_____	Introduction creatively places the student in the story and explains findings	_____
_____	More than two artifacts are explained and inferences made about the Iceman's life and death (explanation and clarity are important here)	_____
_____	Conclusion sums up and explains the student's theory as to who the Iceman was and what happened to him	_____
_____	Postscript, with newest information and student evaluation of the class	_____

Figure 7.7

What Have Archaeologists Learned About the Iceman?

- He lived in a small farming village with some domesticated animals. The village was south of the Alps.
- He worked with the others in planting and hunting, making tools and clothing, and he smelted copper.
- He was approximately 45 years old when he died.
- His last 48 hours were very violent and involved a battle with perhaps four people.
- The Iceman died from an arrow wound. The shooter was below him and perhaps 30 yards behind him.

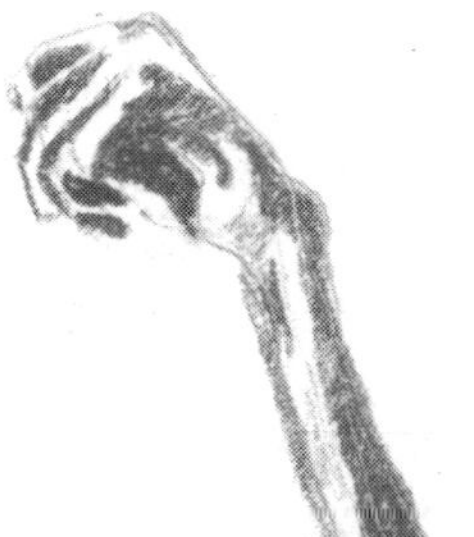

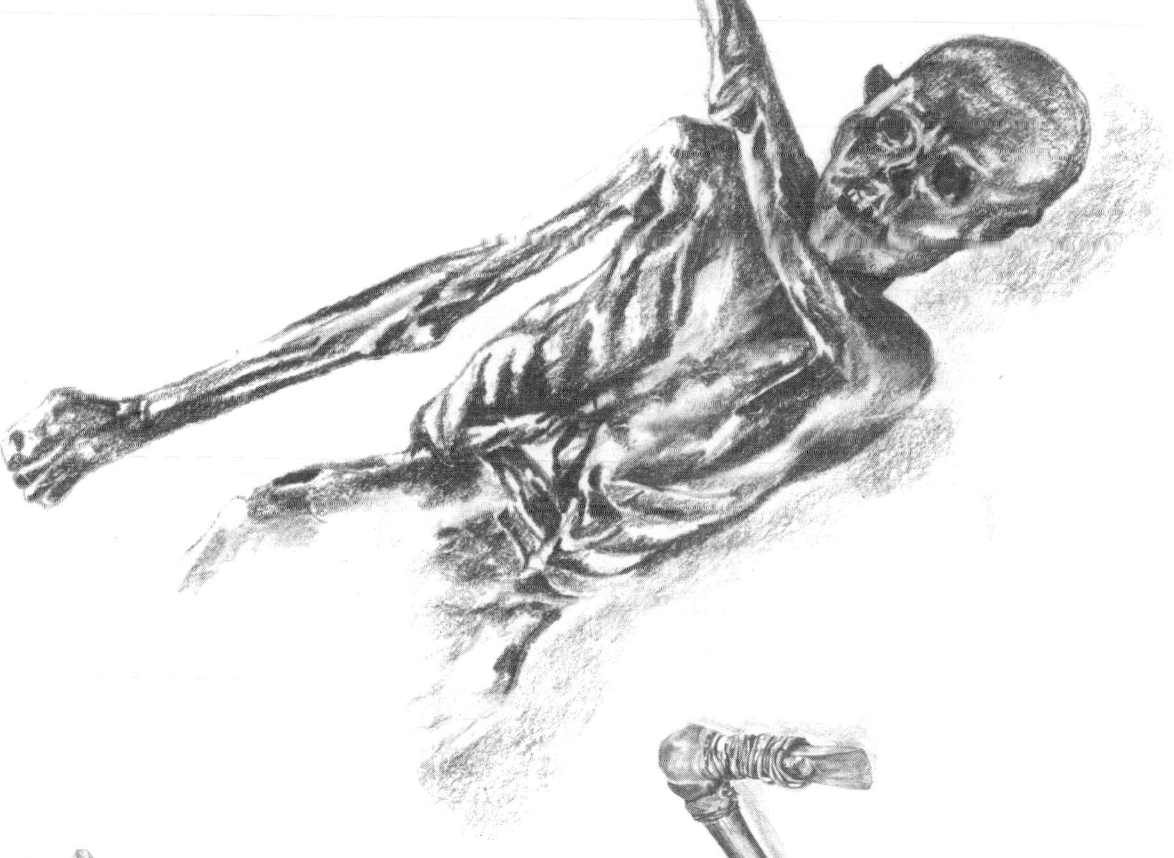

Another way to conclude this lesson is to show portions of *Iceman: Hunt for a Killer*, a Discovery Channel production. This is an excellent program and allows students to visually interact with the ideas that they have been discussing, and see how archaeologists think about the Iceman and what he teaches us.

Depending upon the time available to the teacher, break up your showing of the video into sections. For example, the teacher might choose a section that shows a reenact of life in the Iceman's village, or shows how an ax is made, or how one survives the winter in the Alps. For each section, students could take notes using a Video Viewing Guide (Chapter 3). A classroom discussion could follow the viewing.

9. I follow this lesson up with an Interactive Lecture on "Exploring Life in Prehistoric Times." Because the students have been working with the Iceman discovery, looking for clues, and thinking like archaeologists, they may be ready to explore other aspects of the lives of these remarkable early people.

Sources

This section builds upon an earlier article, Michael M. Yell, "The Time Before History: Thinking Like an Archaeologist," *Social Education* 62, no. 1 (January 1998): 27-31.

Lesson 2: The Roman Antecedents of the Constitution

Western civilization rests upon a continuity of history that runs from ancient Athens and Rome to modern day America. Within that continuity there is a thread, albeit a broken one, that leads to democracy. In this lesson students will read and listen to primary source quotations in order to discover the thread in ancient Athens and Rome that extends to our Constitution. In addition to using these sources, students will examine the concept of civic responsibility in Athens, Rome, and contemporary America. This lesson is part of a seventh grade unit on the Roman Republic.

Outcomes

1. The learner will read and analyze primary sources in order to understand the Roman antecedents of the principal of separation of powers.
2. The learner will compare and contrast the government of ancient Rome, during the republic, with the government of the United States.

Teaching Strategies

- Timed/Pair/Share and Think/Pair/Share (Chapter 2)
- Response Groups (Chapter 2)
- Interactive Lecture (Chapter 2)

Time

Two to three class periods.

Resources

- Excerpts, provided below, given to students as handouts or shown on an overhead projection
- An image (slide, transparency, or illustration in a textbook) of the Roman senate

Procedures

1. Timed/Pair/Share: Tell students, "Explain to your partner what you know about the government of the United States." Then review and discuss with the class what students know about the American form of government.

2. Explain to students, "Today we will look at the government of ancient Rome, and compare it to the government of the United States. Specifically we will be looking at ideas that might have led to the development of our government. We are going to do this by looking at primary sources."

3. Do the "Plebian/Patrician" experiential exercise from the *History Alive!* unit on Ancient Rome. In this exercise most of the class become plebeians and work on a task (usually, cutting up paper into small strips for later use in creating mosaics). A few students become patricians, and these upper class aristocrats are allowed to play games. Often some of the "plebeians" will eventually decide to strike; if they do not I get someone to instigate a strike. This represents an action taken in Rome just prior to the advent of the Roman Republic.

4. Pass out the speech given by Menenius, who may have negotiated the end to the strike (figure 7.8). Explain to students: "This is a speech from the early republic given by Menenius that was supposedly given in 494 BCE. The masses were angry due to being mistreated by creditors, so they withdrew their labor from the city. Menenius was dispatched to persuade them to return."

5. Think/Pair/Share: What was the purpose of this story? Discuss the meaning of this, making reference to metaphors that they may have learned in their language arts class. The plebeians would end the strike provided they had a greater say in the way they were governed.

6. To add visual elements to the discussion show an image (slide, transparency, or illustration in a textbook) of the Roman Senate and ask "What is happening in this picture?" "Does this remind you of anything in our government?" Briefly mention that it is an artist's conception of the Roman Senate. Ask, "What does the Senate do in the United States?"

7. For the next section of the lesson, the teacher utilizes strategy Response Groups to explore and discuss the resulting Roman government structure and how its basic ideas found their way into our constitutional structures. In groups of four, students are given several information sheets to read and discuss. Each information sheet contains primary source statements, pictures, and open-ended reflection questions.

8. The first information sheet has excerpts from the writings of a Polybius. Explain that Polybius was a Roman historian who lived from approximately 204 to 102 BCE. He wrote about the ideas behind the structures of the Roman Republic in one of his books. Put on the Polybius transparency (figure 7.9) and go through a portion of it in class. Have the groups work on the remainder of the information sheet. After coming to a consensus, they are to put the answers in their notebooks.

Figure 7.8

Menenius Speech

In the days when the organs and body parts did not all agree amongst themselves, as is now the case, but had each its own ideas and a voice of its own, the other parts thought it unfair that they should have the worry and the trouble and the labor of providing the food for the stomach, while the stomach remained quietly in their midst with nothing to do but to enjoy the good food; they therefore conspired together that the hands should carry no food to the mouth, nor the mouth accept anything that was given it, nor the teeth grind up what they received. While they sought to starve the stomach into submission, the members themselves and the whole body were reduced to the utmost weakness. Hence it had become clear that even the stomach had no idle task to perform, and was no more nourished than it nourished the rest, by giving out to all parts of the body that by which we live and thrive.

Figure 7.9

Excerpts from Polybius

There are three ways of running a government, which are *kingship, aristocracy,* and *democracy.* We regard the best government as one that partakes of all of these elements. Absolute power rests in no single body.

The consuls are closest to kingship. Our consuls, in addition to leading out the legions, are the masters of administration. In preparations for war, they have all but absolute power.

The Senate has control of the treasury and regulates all payments and receipts. They authorize payment for the care of public buildings and they try all crimes.

The people finally, are the court that decides matters of life and death and money. It is the people who bestow offices on the deserving. All citizens serve on the Assembly.

Discuss the question: why did Polybius feel that the power of government must be divided and how did the Romans divide these powers? Write three or four sentences justifying your answer.

Figure 7.10

Excerpts from *The Federalist Papers* Number 47 and 51

Number 47 — No political truth is...of greater...value, or is more stamped with the authority of liberty....The accumulation of all powers, legislative, executive, and judiciary, in the same hands... may justly be pronounced the very definition of tyranny. ...The preservation of liberty requires that these great departments of power should be separate and distinct....

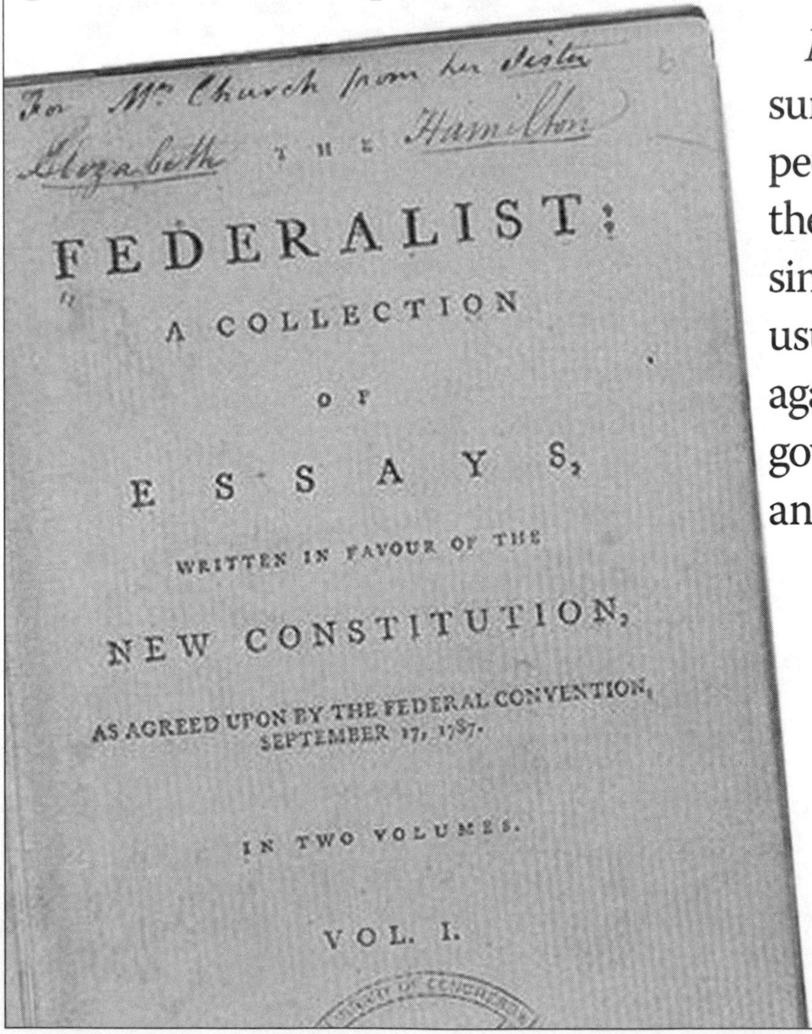

Number 51 — Power surrendered by the people is submitted to the administration of a single government, and the usurpations are guarded against by a division of the government into distinct and separate departments....

Discuss the similarities that existed between the ideas of government of the Roman Republic and the ideas explained in these excerpts from *The Federalist Papers* and the Constitution. Write three or four sentences that explain these similarities.

Figure 7.11

Excerpt from the U. S. Constitution

We the people of the United States, in order to form a more perfect union, establish justice, insure domestic tranquility, provide for the common defense, promote the general welfare, and secure the blessings of liberty to ourselves and our posterity, do ordain and establish this Constitution for the United States of America.

9. With the entire class make a list of phrases and words that Polybius used to describe the Roman government. Discuss and build upon this list. Put on the transparency of the Roman government (under the Republic) and discuss. Have students read the portion of their text that explains the structure of Roman government (or supply a reading). Discuss the questions on the information sheet with the entire class.

10. In this final portion of the lesson, students will examine how the governmental structures of ancient Rome compare to and were antecedents for modern American government. Pass out the information sheet (figure 7.10) with excerpts from *The Federalist Papers* number 47 and 51. After reading the quotations, students discuss the similarities between the two governments.

Following the small group discussion and individual writing on the similarities, once again bring the discussion to the entire class.

11. Closure: The lesson is brought to closure with an Interactive Lecture (see Chapter 2). The Interactive Lecture utilizes a variety of processing strategies and different forms of media (e.g., slides, short video clips) in order to involve students with the content being presented. The purpose is to synthesize, summarize, and deliver information to students while keeping them actively thinking, reflecting, and processing. The outline for the lecture follows:

I. Roman Government
   A. Plebeians and Patricians
   B. Development of the Republic
   C. Polybius and the "mixed constitution"
II. American Government
   A. *The Federalist Papers*
   B. The separation of powers

Every seven to ten minutes of the lecture, pause for student processing. Slides and short video clips could be used to illustrate and augment the main ideas. The teacher could ask students to discuss the images.

12. The end of the lecture (and the lesson) involves looking at part of the preamble of the U. S. Constitution (figure 7.11). Students have now learned about some of the governmental ideas of the Roman republic and the similarity of these ideas with our constitutional principle of separation of powers. In the lecture, challenge students to bring the various parts of the lesson together.

Students can conclude with observations about the Roman/American "exchange of ideas" across the centuries.

Sources

The early portion of the lesson comes from "Patricians and Plebeians: Experiencing a Struggle for Power," in *Ancient Rome*, a *History Alive!* unit of study developed by the Teachers Curriculum Institute (www.historyalive.com). There are a number of excellent Internet sources that were used in the creation of this lesson. Two excellent web resources on Polybius are thelatinlibrary.com/law/polybius.html and www.sms.org/mdl-indx/polybius/polybius.htm. For the Federalist Papers and the Constitution, visit www.ourdocuments.gov.

Lesson 3: What Really Happened on Lexington Green?

This lesson is designed to introduce students in an American Studies class to the process of "doing" history. Students analyze primary and secondary sources—including accounts by rebel eyewitnesses, a British eyewitness, a contemporary writer, a modern historian, and an author of historical fiction—as they attempt to reconstruct what happened on Lexington Green on the morning of April 19, 1775. During the process, students will identify discrepancies between the different accounts, attempt to identify the nature of the writer of each passage, apply a few criteria for determining the credibility of sources, render an interpretation about the event in the face of conflicting evidence, and justify their judgments.

Objectives
Following this lesson, students will be able to:
1. Distinguish eyewitness, contemporary, and historical accounts.
2. Identify several criteria for determining the bias and credibility of sources.
3. Interrogate (i.e., analyze and evaluate) a primary document.
4. Interpret conflicting evidence and then synthesize multiple perspectives into defensible judgments.

Teaching Strategies
- Conceptual Continuum (Chapter 5)
- Discrepant Event Inquiry
- Media K-W-L (Chapter 1)
- RAFT (Chapter 3)

Time
This is a 1- to 2-day lesson (depending on block schedule, student reading level, etc.).

Resources
- Five accounts of the same historical event, as provided in Handout 1.
- Five sources (author and publication) of each account, on a separate sheet of paper (step 7 on page 75).
- Five placards (index cards will do) with the name of an author (p. 75) on each.
- Listening guide for taking notes during debriefing.
- VCR and overhead projector.
- Videotape of the musical 1776 (to serve as a "media hook"). Produced by Columbia Pictures, Riverside, CA, 1972, 148 min.

Procedures
1. Before students arrive, set up four meeting areas in the classroom in a horseshoe pattern.

2. Assign students to one of the four groups as they first enter the classroom.

3. The teacher could construct a Discrepant Event Inquiry (Chapter 2) to use at this point in the lesson. Alternatively, show a brief clip of the scene in the video of the musical 1776 in which performers, acting as eyewitnesses to an event that has just occurred, both glorify and lament the skirmish of April 19, 1775. The teacher then asks: What clues in the scene suggest a time, event, and place? What seems to have happened? What feelings are evoked? This Media K-W-L should elicit students' prior knowledge about the event.

4. Distribute Handout 1, which provides five different accounts of what happened on Lexington Green on April 19, 1775. (The author and source of each account are not listed on that handout.)

5. Inform students that the movie clip and handout refer to the famous engagement at Lexington Green on April 19, 1775 between British troops and colonists. Instruct each group to discuss this question: "What really happened on Lexington Green?" Allow students to silently read the five different accounts. Some of these excerpts contain phrases that require time and effort for modern readers to understand, so invite students to underline phrases or sentences that they do not understand on first reading. Each group can list discrepancies between the five accounts. If students need guidance, the teacher could ask questions such as:
- How many soldiers were present on each side?
- Were the colonists in a line or in an unorganized crowd?
- Why did someone fire a gun? Was there any provocation?
- Who fired first?
- Did the British soldiers behave honorably? Did the American colonists?

The different authors would answer these questions in various ways.

Document 1

On the nineteenth of April instant, about one or two o'clock in the morning, being informed that...a body of regulars were marching from Boston towards Concord,...we were alarmed and having met at the place of our company's parade (Lexington Green), were dismissed by our Captain, John Parker, for the present, with orders to be ready to attend at the beat of the drum, we further testify and declare, that about five o'clock in the morning, hearing our drum beat, we proceeded towards the parade, and soon found that a large body of troops were marching towards us, some of our company were coming up to the parade, and others had reached it, at which time the company began to disperse, whilst our backs were turned on the troops, we were fired on by them, and a number of our men were instantly killed and wounded, not a gun was fired by any person in our company on the regulars to our knowledge before they fired on us, and they continued firing until we had made all our escape.

Document 2

Major Pitcairn screamed at us: "Lay down your arms, you lousy bastards! Disperse, you lousy peasant scum!"...At least, those were the words that I seem to remember. Others remembered differently; but the way he screamed, in his strange London accent, with the motion and excitement, with his horse rearing and kicking...with the drums beating again and the fixed bayonets glittering in the sunshine, it's a wonder that any of his words remain with us.... We still stood in our two lines, our guns butt end on the ground or held loosely in our hands. Major Pitcairn spurred his horse and raced between the lines. Somewhere, away from us, a shot sounded. A redcoat soldier raised his musket, leveled it at Father, and fired. My father clutched at his breast, then crumpled to the ground like an empty sack.... Then the whole British front burst into a roar of sound and flame and smoke.

Document 3

19th. At 2 o'clock we began our march by wading through a very long ford up to our middles; after going a few miles we took three or four people who were going off to give intelligence; about five miles on this side of a town called Lexington, which lay in our road, we heard there were some hundreds of people collected together intending to oppose us and stop our going on; at 5 o'clock we arrived there, and saw a number of people, I believe between 200 and 300, formed in a common in the middle of the town; we still continued advancing, keeping prepared against an attack though without intending to attack them; but on our coming near them they fired one or two shots, upon which our men without any orders, rushed in upon them, fired and put them to flight; several of them were killed, we could not tell how many, because they were got behind walls and into the woods; We had a man of the 10th light Infantry wounded, nobody else hurt. We then formed on the Common, but with some difficulty, the men were so wild they could hear no orders; we waited a considerable time there, and at length proceeded on our way to Concord.

Document 4

There is a certain sliding over and indeterminateness in describing the beginning of the firing. Major Pitcairn who was a good man in a bad cause, insisted upon it to the day of his death, that the colonists fired first...He does not say that he saw the colonists fire first. Had he said it, I would have believed him, being a man of integrity and honor. He expressly says he did not see who fired first; and yet believed the peasants began. His account is this— that riding up to them he ordered them to disperse; which they not doing instantly, he turned about to order his troops so to draw out as to surround and disarm them. As he turned he saw a gun in a peasant's hand from behind a wall, flash in the pan without going off; and instantly or very soon two or three guns went off by which he found his horse wounded and also a man near him wounded. These guns he did not see, but believing they could not come from his own people, doubted not and so asserted that they came from our people; and that thus they began the attack. The impetuosity of the King's Troops were such that a promiscuous, uncommanded but general fire took place, which Pitcairn could not prevent; though he struck his staff or sword downwards with all earnestness as a signal to forbear or cease firing. This account Major Pitcairn himself gave Mr. Brown of Providence who was seized with flour and carried to Boston a few days after the battle; and Gov. Sessions told it to me.

Document 5

In April 1775, General Gage, the military governor of Massachusetts, sent out a body of troops to take possession of military stores at Concord, a short distance from Boston. At Lexington, a handful of "embattled farmers," who had been tipped off by Paul Revere, barred the way. The "rebels" were ordered to disperse. They stood their ground. The English fired a volley of shots that killed eight patriots. It was not long before the swift-riding Paul Revere spread the news of this new atrocity to the neighboring colonies. The patriots of all New England, although still a handful, were now to fight the English.

6. List on the board in front of the class the five different "profiles" of the authors of the five different accounts:
- a rebel eyewitnesses,
- a British eyewitness,
- a contemporary writer,
- a modern historian, and
- an author of historical fiction.

Ask students to try to pair each author with his or her respective statement. Allow 10 minutes for students to discuss their choices with other members of their group, and to change their choices if they wish.

7. Discuss some of their choices with the students, then announce the correct author for each passage, by reading aloud:

The passage that begins:	was written by:
"On the nineteenth April instant ..."	Nathaniel Mulliken and 33 other minutemen, in testimony given on April 25, 1775 before three justices of the peace.
"Major Pitcairn screamed at us ..."	Howard Fast in his novel *April Morning* of 1961 (Toronto: Bantam Books, 1961)
"At 2 o'clock we began our march ..."	British Lieutenant John Barker, diary entry for April 19, 1775.
"There is a certain sliding over ..."	Ezra Stiles, president of Yale College, diary entry for August 21, 1775.
"In April 1775, General Gage ..."	S. Steinberg, in *The United States, Story of a Free People*, a textbook from 1963.

8. Ask each group to rank order the five documents in terms of credibility. Ask one group to stand in the front of the room in a continuum in which they hold up placards for each of the five authors, ranking them from least to most credible. Invite disagreement from other groups. As the discussion proceeds, the teacher can ask the following questions:
- Why do some of these accounts seem to be more credible than others?

- How confident are you in ranking the authors this way?
- What else would you like to know that would increase your confidence in the accuracy of information in any one of the documents.

9. Closure. Inform students of their homework assignment (see assessments below) and/or ask them to complete an exit slip before they leave. Possible questions include:
- What happened on Lexington Green?
- What is an eyewitness? A contemporary? A historian?
- How would you determine the credibility of ... (fill in a local scenario with which students are familiar)?

10. Possible assessments:
- Elaborated written communication. Provide students with two historians' accounts—one American and one British—of what happened on Lexington Green. Ask students to "interrogate" each document (e.g., "list 3-5 questions ...") and to render a "qualified judgment" concerning the events of April 19, 1775, given what these historians say, in light of what was considered in class today.
- Students assume the role of a colonial alderman and write a letter to a neighboring Committee of Correspondence, detailing what happened at Lexington and rallying concern about British tactics, then write a response from a Loyalist perspective (e.g., a letter from colonial entrepreneur to a Company official in London).
- Give students three additional accounts of the affair; ask them to predict who wrote them and/or tell students who wrote them and ask which seems most credible and why;
- Now "interrogate" one of these documents. What would you like to know that would increase your confidence in assessing the credibility of the statement? Jot down at least three questions.

Source

Based on the longer and more elaborate lesson plan in Geoffrey Scheurman, "Revisiting Lexington Green," *Social Education* 62, no. 1 (January 1998): 10-17.

Lesson 4: Fundamentalism and Modernism in The Scopes Monkey Trial

Students examine the social and political climate underlying the "Scopes Monkey Trial" of 1925. Using a number of strategies (viewing, reading, discussion, and writing), students discover and develop a conceptual continuum that captures the social, political, and psychological forces that were responsible for the spirit of the times. They then apply this new knowledge to historical artifacts and modern examples of the debate, as it manifests itself today, over the teaching of evolution in public schools.

Objectives

The learner will

1. Describe the "conceptual forces" at work in the United States during the Scopes Monkey Trial.
2. Interpret other historical events, as seen in specific artifacts, in light of this new knowledge.
3. Develop a budding sense of "argument," including evaluation of a contemporary issue using the insights gained from this investigation.

Teaching Strategies

- Conceptual Continuum (Chapter 5)
- Philosophical Chairs (Chapter 5)

Time

From two to five class periods.

Resources

Several specific resources are listed here. However, numerous other products will serve equally well as curricular materials. The resourceful teacher will identify the videotapes, readings, and primary documents best suited to his or her students.

- A video documentary of the Scopes Monkey Trial— The History Channel's *In Search of History: The Scopes Monkey Trial*—is ideal.[1] PBS has also released an episode of *American Experience*, "The Monkey Trial.")[2] Questar Video has produced a tape titled *Headline Stories of the Century: A Newsreel Library of America in The News*, which contains a very brief segment on the Scopes Trial (among many other events).[3]
- A general secondary text on the trial at an appropriate reading level and containing enough detail to create "concept pairs" such as those described below. I recommend the Famous Trials website maintained at the University of Kentucky by Doug Linder (www.law.umkc.edu/faculty/projects/ftrials/scopes/scopes.htm). However, various sites also house useful secondary information, replicas of primary documents, and

links to other sites. Among a few of my favorites:
- xroads.virginia.edu/~UG97/inherit/1925home.html
- www.dimensional.com/~randl/scopes.htm
- www.pbs.org/wgbh/amex/monkeytrial/
- www3.mistral.co.uk/bradburyac/tennesse.html
- dir.yahoo.com/Government/Law/Cases/Scopes_Monkey_Trial/
- www.christianitytoday.com/ct/2000/006/2.50.html
- Student handouts, including a Viewing Guide and a Reading Guide (or other items as determined by the amount of scaffolding necessary).
- Follow-up materials for applying and extending the lesson (as determined by teacher).

Procedures

Assuming that students have a little prior knowledge about the 1920s in general, here is a sequence of six steps for introducing the Monkey Trial, with an eye toward uncovering the underlying "world views" at the heart of the controversy.

Step 1. Dayton, Tennessee, 1925. Extrapolating prevailing views from context

A. Objective: To recognize "conceptual forces" at work in historical context

B. Materials: Video documentary, *The Scopes Monkey Trial*

C. Activity: The History Channel video documentary *The Scopes Monkey Trial* begins with a lively overview of the "jazz age," complete with historical footage showing dramatic changes at work during the decade. After this review of the context, the film's focus then moves quickly to "the quiet town" of Dayton, Tennessee. As they watch the drama unfold, students are asked to jot down anything— persons, events, organizations, and ideas—that may foreshadow or reflect "opposing forces at work in the world." The goal is not for them to spend inordinate amounts of time taking notes, but rather to make quick observations on a Video Viewing Guide (Chapter 3). It is critical that the teacher pauses early and often, to model for the students what is meant by "opposing forces" or "dichotomous world views" (see discussion and examples in Chapter 5). In this way, "conceptual categories" are formed early in the process and students can be looking for additional entries almost immediately. The teacher may invoke Think-Pair-Share or other processing strategies in between segments, so long as students' lists of opposing forces grow as they watch more of the video.

D. Performance: After a sufficient number of entries are collected for each opposing "perspective," the teacher asks students to "elaborate" in one of several ways. For example, students may take the words from each perspective and compose a Sentence Synthesis for each list. Whatever the teacher decides, student samples are shared and the class arrives at a consensus on what terms to use to describe the opposite poles of the dichotomy (e.g., "Fundamentalism" and "Modernism"—see discussion in Chapter 5).

Step 2. Headline Stories: deriving naïve arguments and reinforcing dichotomies

A. Objective: To develop a naïve sense of "argument" while reinforcing the conceptual categories established in Session 1.

B. Materials: Newsreel footage from The History Channel's "In Search of History: The Monkey Trial" (the same objective can be met with political cartoons or other materials if this video is unavailable).

C. Activity: In the spirit of a Response Group (see Chapter 2), three-person teams imagine they are sitting in a movie theatre in 1925 when a short newsreel summarizes the events in Dayton, Tennessee. Tell the class that during the "Intermission" of the feature presentation (a Charlie Chaplin movie), they will be standing in the concession line together when a vigorous debate breaks out. One person in the group is designated as an avowed "Fundamentalist" and watches the Newsreel from that perspective. Another is an avowed "Modernist" and the third is an undecided bystander. Show the clip and immediately have the debate between two people break out. The bystander is responsible for keeping notes and, later, revealing what the key points were in the debate. The teacher probes students to establish what distinguishes an intellectual "argument" from a mere "shouting match."

D. Performance: Some individuals participate in a spontaneous but somewhat informed debate while others must develop a synopsis of what they heard and summarize it for the class. The teacher reinforces the Conceptual Continuum with questions and comments about the disagreements that emerged from the various debates. This is also an opportune time to introduce students to the concept of "argument" itself. There are myriad ways

to treat this topic. I especially like the conceptualization for diagramming arguments offered by Steven Toulmin.[4] However, the key here is to insure that students at least have a sense of the difference between a "fact" and a "claim" and develop an awareness and appreciation for how an argument is constructed and communicated.

Step 3. Famous Trials: Adding content to concept

A. Objective: To add substance and complexity to the dichotomy through focused reading on secondary textual material.

B. Materials: The Scopes Concepts List (Student Handout A on p. 81), the Scopes Trial Reading Guide (Student Handout B on p. 82), and a standard secondary historical reading on the trial with sufficient detail (beyond that in the video) to be interesting.

C. Activity: Ask students to take two colored highlighters and mark the reading in terms of the opposing perspectives already established in Steps 1-2 (this also makes a simple but focused homework assignment). Then, in Response Group format, have 2-3 student teams categorize their conceptual pairs on a piece of paper, like Student Handout B (students may not think to "invent" opposite terms or categories for some of the specific references in the reading, so the teacher may scaffold this part of the activity by modeling a response). This is a variation on the Anticipation Guide idea (Chapter 4).

After this is complete, the teacher distributes concepts (words or phrases) that she has extrapolated from the reading (Student Handout A). Members of each team shuffle the words until they have created thirteen opposing pairs. To add an additional thinking component to this activity, the teacher may ask students to denote the "degree of dichotomy" between pairs by how far apart they place them on the continuum. For example, "fundamentalist" and "modernist" might be spread far apart whereas "north" and "south" might remain closer together in the context of the Scopes trial.

D. Performance: Discuss the pairs formed on the handout. For example, the teacher might pull conceptual terms from a hat, ask spokespeople from different teams to offer a paired concept and then discuss why it represents a dichotomy in the context of the Scopes trial. The teacher can probe students for their understanding of the material, invite disagreement, compare the degree of dichotomy among conceptual pairs, and so on. Also, this is a good time to insert additional information as the discussion about conceptual pairs segues into an Interactive Lecture.

Step 4. Document Analysis: Straight from the horse's mouth (or pen or brush)

A. Objective: To encounter the conceptual continuum "in the raw," as it appears in primary documents created during the period.

B. Materials: Select at least three different sources, two of which students can clearly identify (with effort) as "fundamentalist" or "modernist" in origin. These might be editorials, political cartoons, or even excerpts from court proceedings (e.g., closing arguments of each attorney). The third document is selected carefully based on one of several criteria. For example, it may be a statement with a more moderate viewpoint that students must analyze carefully to determine its "leaning." Or, it may be a statement written by an author who seeks to find common ground by synthesizing both views. Finally, it may be a document whose author pushes the envelope by offering a point of view that simply doesn't "fit" the dichotomy (a creative third alternative).

C. Activity: Students perform a cursory "comparative analysis" of the three documents as indicated on the Reading Guide (Handout B). Encourage them to place each document on the continuum between "most fundamental" and "most modern" and then answer the questions in the handout. The teacher then assigns one of the three documents to each group, which analyzes it in more detail, as indicated on the handout. The debriefing of the handout involves spokespeople responding from each group in the form of a Response Group. Depending on time, a variation on this procedure is for each group to analyze one document, followed by debriefing, then repeat this process for each of the other documents, so that each group analyzes every document.

D. Performance: Interrogating primary sources is one of the most important skills students should practice. Performance on this activity allows the teacher to make explicit the kinds of questions and processes a historian uses to analyze the raw materials of history: What would you like to know about the author? Once you know something, what does this say about the author's credibility? Who was his audience? How would you go about verifying accuracy? What is the timing of the document's publication (before or after a specific event)? What prejudices might the student himself bring to the document? Once again, the discussion that follows the reading of these documents is the most critical piece in guiding student performance to uncover important conceptual ideas.

Step 5. Inherit the Wind: *The argument updated and portrayed*

A. Objective: To reinforce students' understanding of the conceptual continuum by examining and then writing about the issue as it appears in a novel context.

B. Materials: A film clip from *Inherit the Wind* based on the screenplay written in 1955. Spencer Tracy stars in a 1960 version.

C. Activity: Prior to the film, students might create Brief Biographies of the colorful characters in the trial (Scopes, Darrow, Bryan, Judge Ralston, H. L. Mencken, etc.). Or, the teacher may set up the clip with a brief Interactive Lecture highlighting the context of the film in general and the clip in particular. Students are also invited to consider issues involving historical fiction and unorthodox judicial practice as well as questions concerning audience, translation, and perspective ("21st century viewers of a 1960 rendition of a 1925 event"). The clip shows the actor playing William Jennings Bryan taking the stand as "an expert on the Bible" and his subsequent examination by Clarence Darrow (Tracy).

NOTE: The teacher may wish to set this lesson up with a more thorough discussion or examples of what constitutes an argument, what argumentative or persuasive writing looks like, and so on. Also, he may want to pause the videotape to highlight certain claims and assumptions or rhetorical "moves" employed by the speakers in the scene. Once students have watched and digested the scene, they are asked to complete a writing assignment in the spirit of the I-Search Essay.

D. Performance: Keeping in mind the previous lessons in this series, students begin (or draft a complete) "closing argument" for the defense and the prosecution in the Scopes Monkey Trial. (Given sufficient explanation, the teacher may wish to have students write this as "opening arguments" at a subsequent appeal of the trial's verdict on constitutional grounds).

This may constitute the culminating activity for this series of lessons or the teacher may add one more step, deepening student understanding even further by having them apply their knowledge to a contemporary situation, namely the debate over evolution in schools today.

Step 6. The Kansas Question Today: The argument revisited

A. Objective: To consider how "conceptual forces" endure.

B. Materials: At least two artifacts (newspaper article, editorial, letter to the editor, government document) pertaining to the ongoing issue concerning the teaching of evolution in schools today. There was much discussion concerning the use of the word "evolution" in Kansas recently, providing ample material for a debate in a modern setting.

C. Activity: The Scopes trial provides an opportunity to employ the Philosophical Chairs discussion strategy. The teacher provides sufficient background information on the particular debate in Kansas as well as any other details necessary to generate the debate. For example, another miniature Interactive Lecture may be in order, detailing the 10th Amendment to the Constitution, the role of state boards in determining curriculum, highlighting precedents involving academic freedom, and so on. Along with some of the more classic statements emanating from different communities of discussion in the nation at large, students will probably have enough "deep background" on the general issues to get into the debate fairly rapidly. The nature of the question used to generate the discussion is, as always with this strategy, of primary importance.

The teacher should be ready to intervene with modified questions to insure an appropriate response. For example, if the discussion topic does not elicit the argumentative atmosphere the teacher is seeking , he or she may introduce a more extreme or controversial topic or question. If statement (i) does not elicit student participation, the teacher may want to shift to statement (ii) or (iii).

> Statement (i): "Actions taken by the Kansas State Board of Regents, regarding removal of 'evolution' from the approved state curriculum, should be protected by the U.S. Constitution."

> Statement (ii): "Local officials should have maximum freedom to choose the public school curriculum in accord with community standards, opinions and beliefs."

> Statement (iii): "Teachers should be free to teach creationism in their science courses."

This activity might serve as a substitute for the *Inherit the Wind* oral argument writing exercise described in Session 5 above. Alternatively, it might also be used as an introduction to the entire series of Monkey Trial lessons, even before students have the background knowledge concerning conflicting ideologies acquired during this unit. Students could then revisit the topic with a repeat version of Philosophical Chairs and/or an I-Search Essay at the end of the series.

D. Performance: As discussed in Chapter 6, the debate itself is designed to elicit a particular performance from students and it can be facilitated in such a way that the teacher can evaluate student understanding (through the ability to conduct an intelligent conversation on the issue). The teacher may also wish to end the debate by asking students to re-create part of the dialogue in written form, capturing at least one key component from both sides of the debate.

Producing and Performing Through Projects

Extensions for this lesson can use the intellectual work completed so far as a spring board for project-based activity involving further research, evaluation, and student enrichment.

Project A: Researching Key Topics

The Monkey Trial serves both as a mirror, reflecting the zeitgeist of the 1920s, and as a force that helped shape contemporary societal attitudes and mores. It captured the imagination of the nation and the world, and invoked responses from communities ranging from scientific to religious, technological to psychological, and academic to jurisprudential. With prevalent resources, here is just a sampling of five core questions that students may consider in their research. These are accompanied by a few exemplary projects that students might pursue in order to develop skills of authentic intellectual work and generalize their knowledge about the Monkey Trial to other domains.

1. TOPIC: THE INFLUENCE OF SPECIFIC INDIVIDUALS

Research Question: Where does the line form between objective news reporting and editorial writing?

Project: Have students read several of H. L. Mencken's reports about the trial and consider their influence on public opinion in various parts of the country. (The same assignment can be done with a particular political cartoonist, many of which had a heyday with the Monkey Trial.) Students should write their own "report" and "editorial" (or oppositional cartoons) on a current issue where fundamentalist and modernist perspectives are apparent.

2. TOPIC: THE INFLUENCE OF TECHNOLOGY

Research Question: This was the first trial broadcast on radio. How did radio change the way Americans formed their opinions?

Project: Have the class re-enact parts of the trial on a tape recorder, complete with "commentary" inserted by "student broadcasters." Then simulate a 1925 setting and have the class sit around the "radio," listen and react. Discuss the issues surrounding the presence of television in courtrooms today.

3. TOPIC: THE INFLUENCE OF SELF-INTEREST

Research Question: What are the possible motives of Scopes, the ACLU, the business leaders in Dayton, Tennessee, and other key players in the trial?

Project: Have students examine how motivations and vested interests influence the drama and outcome of an event. Studens can construct a scenario where the motives of the actors change and the outcome of the trial therefore changes as well. Or, they can consider a contemporary newsworthy event and predict the outcome given particular motives of the key players involved.

4. TOPIC: THE INFLUENCE OF EDUCATION

Research Question: How is the issue of evolutionism and creationism handled in your school?

Project: Have students examine the actual curriculum in Tennessee, then examine local curriculum guides and interview teachers and members of their own community. Students can develop a poster of "comparisons and contrasts" in the curriculum and the issues from then and now. They can then present the poster to the rest of the class.

5. TOPIC: THE INFLUENCE OF COMMON LAW

Research Question: What influence does an "opinion" of an appellate court have on the evolution of a historical trend?

Project: Have different students investigate the particulars surrounding particular court cases (e.g., *Epperson v. Arkansas*, 1968), including the context, arguments, court opinions, and societal impact of the case. Have students re-enact the oral arguments from a famous Supreme Court case (in age-appropriate language), then deliver the majority and dissenting opinions of the court (also in translated form).

Continued on page 83

Scopes Concepts List

Match up these 26 terms into 13 pairs, each of which reveals part of the controversy of the Scopes Monkey Trial or the societal divisions that fueled the controversy.

American Civil Liberties Union (ACLU)

Agnosticism

Anti-Evolution League

Bigotry

Clarence Darrow

Creationism

Evolution

Fundamentalism

Gospel

Hell and the High School

Jazz

John T. Scopes v.

Literal

Metaphorical

Modernism

North

Origin of Species

Religion

Rural

Science

South

State of Tennessee

Tolerance

Traditionalist

Urban

William Jennings Bryan

Scopes Trial Reading Guide

Using information from the video and readings, fill in the boxes below, listing at least TWO key people, as well as names of groups, books, organizations or other perspectives that supported each "side" of the controversy. Finally, summarize the basic "argument" for each side of the issue (Hint: a strong argument needs more than a simple "claim," and, it must also include reasons and evidence.)

Side One   **Side Two**

   Individuals or Groups: Individuals or Groups:

   Books, films, documents, etc.:   Books, films, documents, etc.:

   Other ideas or perspectives: Other ideas or perspectives:

   Summary of basic argument: Summary of basic argument:

2. Refer to the Scopes Concepts List, with 13 pairs of opposing terms. Write down TWO pairs of opposing terms that you think best summarize what the dispute was all about.

Side One   **Side Two**

3. Go back and find three additional idea pairs in the reading for both sides of the argument.

Project B: Multiple document analysis
Students can consider the three documents provided by the teacher (see p. 78, Step 4). Who do they think wrote (spoke or drew) each one? Students can either identify a specific person or else describe a "type" of person (political affiliation, particular motivation, occupation, group member, etc.)?

Document A: _____
    What makes you think it was this person or type of person (specific evidence from text)?

Document B: _____
    What makes you think it was this person or type of person (specific evidence from text)?

Document C: _____
    What makes you think it was this person or type of person (specific evidence from text)?

    Now rate the documents on a scale from "modernist" to "fundamentalist."

MOST MODERNIST   MOST FUNDAMENTALIST

◄─────────────────────────────────►

Project C: Single -document analysis
Assign a single document for students to look at in depth. They should construct some hypotheses about the timing, audience, motivations, and consequences of the document and offer at least one significant question about it.
    Hypothesis 1 (when, to whom, for what reason): _____
    Hypothesis 2: _____
    Question: _____

    The teacher reveals who created each of the documents and provides information to answer the questions: when? to whom? and for what reason? Students should focus on the impact they think such a statement had on others (in the courtroom, in Tennessee, in the nation, in the media) and provide specific reasoning to support their interpretations.

    Document _____
    Who? _____
    To Whom? _____
    When? _____
    Why? _____

Play the section of the video that shows Darrow making the case for the defense. Ask students to imagine that they are the defense attorney and that the trial is almost over. Ask them to "Write at least five sentences of your closing arguments." (For additional credit, they can also create the first five sentences of the prosecuting attorney's closing arguments.) Evaluate the statements based on how well students capture the essence of each "point of view"—or argument—that they have been constructing throughout this exercise.

DEFENSE   PROSECUTION
(Scopes / Darrow)   (Tennessee / Bryan)

◄─────────────────────────────────►

Notes
1. *In Search of History: The Monkey Trial* (New York: The History Channel, 1996, 50 min.)
2. *American Experience: The Monkey Trial* (Alexandria, VA: PBS, 2002, 60 min.)
3. *Headline Stories of the Century: A Newsreel Library of America in the News* (Chicago: Questar Video, 1992, 90 min.)
4. Steven Toulmin, *An Introduction to Reasoning* (New York: Macmillan, 1978).

CHAPTER 8

Resources

The strategies and ideas we have presented were adapted from a variety of sources, including books, articles, university courses, workshops, and discussions with colleagues. We developed variations on these strategies in our classrooms and collected examples of specific applications that worked. In this final chapter, we list and annotate some of the resources that we feel would be most helpful for teachers who wish to expand their repertoire of engaging teaching strategies or to read more about on the basic strategies presented here.

Benjamin, Amy. *Writing in the Content Areas*. Larchmont, NY: Eye On Education, 1999. www.eyeoneducation.com

This teacher-friendly book examines how teachers can utilize writing in various disciplines. The emphasis is not on writing as an add-on activity but as an effective way to teach the content itself. As teachers of history and social studies, we often assign essays, term papers, and other writing tasks to our students. This book provides strategies and tips for teachers to help students improve their writing.

Billmeyer, Rachel, and Barton, Mary Lee. *Teaching Reading in the Content Areas: If Not Me Then Who?* Aurora, CO: McREL (Mid-continent Regional Educational Library), 1998. www.mcrel.org

This book contains forty reading strategies to help student improve their comprehension of what they read. Each entry contains a general description of a strategy and the procedures for using it.

Bower, Burt, Jim Lobdell, and Lee Swenson, *History Alive! Teaching Students in the Diverse Classroom*. Palo Alto, CA: Teachers' Curriculum Institute, 1999. www.historyalive.com

These authors have created excellent commercial materials for history teachers. *History Alive!* contains clear explanations of eight interactive and engaging teaching strategies that interest and engage students. TCI also develops classroom materials for World and American history courses at the middle and secondary levels, and is creating materials for young students that follow the "expanding horizons" approach to elementary social studies.

Bruce, William C. and Jean K. Bruce. *Mindtronics*. Tyler, TX: Home Tree Media, 2002. www.wcbruce.org

In the early 1990s, Bill and Jean Bruce published *Teaching Social Studies with Discrepant Event Inquiry*. Although this book is no longer in print, it has been expanded and reissued as an e-book, *Mindtronics*, which can be purchased at the Bruces' web page and downloaded onto your computer (you will also receive a CD by mail). A review of this e-book, "Inquiry with an E-Book: A Natural Strategy for Social Studies," by Michael M. Yell, was published in *Social Education* 66, no. 3 (April 2002), pp. 184-185.

Buehl, Doug. *Classroom Strategies for Interactive Learning*. Schofield, WI: Wisconsin State Reading Association, 1995.

This book is a guide to many teaching strategies that have the aim of helping students better understand what they read. Written by a teacher, this book is about as teacher-friendly as they come.

Eggen, Paul and Donald Kauchak. *Strategies for Teachers: Teaching Content and Thinking Skills*. Boston, MA: Allyn and Bacon, 1996. www.abacon.com

This book is an important resource for social studies and history teachers of all levels who wish to expand their repertoire of active teaching strategies. Moving from a discussion of models of teaching based on information processing, teacher effectiveness research, and active teaching, the authors guide their readers through various strategies covering such topics as inductive reasoning, concept-attainment, inquiry-based direct instruction, and cooperative learning.

Harmin, Merrill. *Strategies to Inspire Active Learning*. Alexandria, VA: Association for Supervision and Curriculum Development, 1993. www.ascd.org

The active teaching strategies in this book will increase the energy level of any class. It contains more than 100 techniques grouped under such headings as "Everyday Instructional Strategies, "Basic Classroom Procedures," and "Stimulating Thinking."

Joyce, Bruce, Marsha Weil, and Emily Calhoun. *Models of Teaching*. Needham Heights, MS: Allyn and Bacon, 2000. www.abacon.com

This book, first published more than thirty years ago, has been revised and reprinted many times. It thoroughly explains research-based teaching strategies and groups them under different "families of teaching models." Some of the strategies discussed in detail are inquiry, concept attainment, Hilda Taba's inductive thinking, and group investigation.

Kagan, Spencer. *Cooperative Learning*. San Clemente, CA: Kagan Cooperative Learning, 1995. www.kagancooplearn.com

Kagan developed the structural approach to cooperative learning. The book is a classic in the field, containing approximately 100 teaching strategies that use cooperative learning, including "Numbered Heads Together," "Think-Pair-Share," "Roundtable," and "Co-op Co-op."

Morton, Tom. *Cooperative Learning and Social Studies: Toward Excellence & Equity*. San Clemente, CA: Kagan Cooperative Learning, 1998. www.kagancooplearn.com

Morton is a social studies teacher who has taken a number of Kagan's cooperative learning strategies and applied them to specific social studies disciplines. He provides numerous examples of how each strategy can be used in the classroom.

Nosich, Gerald M. *Learning to Think Things Through: A Guide to Critical Thinking in the Curriculum.* Upper Saddle River, NJ: Prentice-Hall, 2001. www.prenhall.com

Nosich is the assistant director at the Center for Critical Thinking and a colleague of Richard Paul. This book, built on Paul's model of critical thinking, was written to help teachers incorporate critical thinking concepts into lesson plans. Among other things, Nosich considers how elements of reasoning and the intellectual standards, so vital for disciplined thinking, can be incorporated into the classroom.

Paul, Richard. *Critical Thinking: How to Prepare Students for a Rapidly Changing World.* Santa Rosa, CA: The Foundation for Critical Thinking, 1993. www.criticalthinking.org

Richard Paul is an international leader in critical thinking. The director of the Center for Critical Thinking at Sonoma State, Paul is a prolific writer and speaker. This book contains dozens of his essays in which he lays out his ideas on how to help our students (and ourselves), learn to engage in disciplined thought, apply our intellectual abilities, and aim for high standards.

Scheurman, Geoffrey, and Michael M. Yell. "Constructing Knowledge in Social Studies," *Social Education* 62, no. 1, January 1998.

This special issue of *Social Education* examined the issues involved in constructing knowledge in the social studies. It deals with constructivist teaching, authentic intellectual work, assessment, and it also discusses strategies used in *History Alive!*

Stahl, Robert, ed. *Cooperative Learning in Social Studies: A Handbook for Teachers.* Menlo Park, CA: Addison-Wesle, 1994. www.awl.com

Stahl, a former president of NCSS, provides a thorough examination of the use of cooperative learning in social studies and history. The book includes articles by such well-known developers, practitioners and trainers as David and Roger Johnson, Spencer Kagan, and the Sharans.

Tompkins, Gail E. *50 Literacy Strategies Step by Step.* Upper Saddle River, NJ: Prentice-Hall, 1998. www.merilleducation.com

This book contains fifty reading and comprehension strategies, including the "Anticipation Guide," "K-W-L Charts," and "Reciprocal Questioning." Each section contains step-by-step procedures for using a strategy as well as examples of its application.

Wineburg, Sam. *Historical Thinking and other Unnatural Acts: Charting the Future of Teaching the Past.* Philadelphia, PA: Temple University Press, 2001. www.temple.edu/tempress

Wineburg's scholarly work examines cognitive and philosophical aspects of learning about history. Of particular interest for secondary history teachers are the sections on "reading historically" and questioning and interrogating primary sources.

Yell, Michael M. "Putting Gel Pen to Paper," *Educational Leadership* 60, no. 3, November 2002. www.ascd.org

This article examines "quick-write" strategies that incorporate writing into daily classroom lessons. In addition to several strategies included in this volume, the article contains others such as "outcome sentences," "frames," and "short statements."

Yell, Michael M. "Multiple Choice to Multiple Rubrics: One Teacher's Journey in Assessment," *Social Education* 63, no. 6, October 1999, 326-329. www.socialstudies.org

This article examines a number of the strategies mentioned in this book (as well as a few that are not), and examines how they can be utilized for assessment.

Web Resources

National Council for the Social Studies
www.socialstudies.org

NCSS is a professional organization for social studies educators. Its website contains a wealth of ideas, materials, opportunities, and collegial support for social studies and history teachers at all levels. NCSS also has affiliate councils in every state.

National Center for History in the Schools
www.sscnet.ucla.edu/nchs

NCHS, located at the University of California at Los Angeles, has published over sixty units of study that are the fruits of collaboration between history professors and experienced teachers. Each unit is based on primary sources and can be purchased as an e-book or as a small booklet.

National Council for History Education
www.history.org/nche

Founded in 1990 as a successor to the Bradley Commission, NCHE is a history advocacy organization with resources for history teachers at all levels.

About the authors

Michael M. Yell is a seventh grade social studies teacher at the Hudson Middle School in Hudson, Wisconsin. In his 28 years in education Mike has received a number of honors for his teaching. He was named Outstanding Social Studies Teacher of the Year (Middle Level) by National Council for the Social Studies (NCSS) in 1998. He received his National Board Certification in 2003. In addition to his teaching, he is an educational writer, and offers seminars and workshops on engaging teaching strategies. He is an active member of NCSS, and was a member of the NCSS board from 2000 to 2003. He is also active in the Wisconsin Council for the Social Studies, for which he has been a board member since 1995. He can be reached at yellmm@hudson. k12.wi.us.

Geoffrey Scheurman is a professor in the Department of Teacher Education at the University of Wisconsin–River Falls, where he teaches undergraduate and graduate courses in Educational Psychology, Techniques of Social Studies Teaching, and the Historical, Philosophical, and Multicultural Foundations of Education. In addition to teaching, Geoff has been the author of many articles and has organized workshops on critical thinking, authentic instruction and assessment, motivation, and constructivist teaching strategies. Before he became a college professor, Geoff worked for 11 years in Wyoming as a middle-secondary social studies and humanities teacher, basketball and track coach, and department chair.

Keith Reynolds teaches high school American history and civics at North High in North Saint Paul, Minnesota. As a new teacher, Keith is well versed in his subject area and theories of teaching and learning, and also understands only too well the need for concrete but adaptable strategies to use in the classroom.

Index

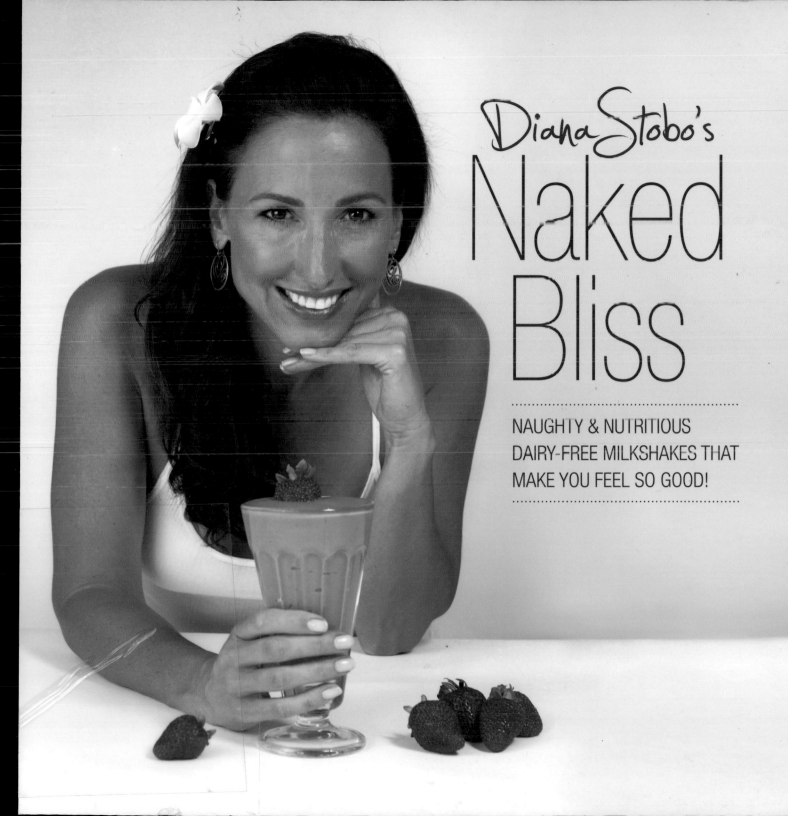

Diana Stobo's
Naked
Bliss

NAUGHTY & NUTRITIOUS
DAIRY-FREE MILKSHAKES THAT
MAKE YOU FEEL SO GOOD!